Maggie Drummond has enjoyed a long and varied media career since she left stockbroking in the early 1970s to become a journalist. She has written for magazines and national newspapers on a wide range of topics including health, fashion and finance as well as being involved in several television productions. She lives in Kent with her husband, well-known stockmarket commentator Michael Walters, and their two children.

NO FUSS
FAT LOSS

MAGGIE DRUMMOND

ORION

An Orion Paperback
First published in Great Britain in 2000 by
Orion Books Ltd,
Orion House, 5 Upper St Martin's Lane,
London WC2H 9EA

Second impression 2001

A CIP catalogue record for this book
is available from the British Library.

ISBN: 0 75283 724 9

Printed and bound in Great Britain by
The Guernsey Press Co. Ltd, Guernsey, C. I.

ACKNOWLEDGEMENTS

I would like to thank my friends Hazel Collins and Martina Nicolls for their inspiration and help with the recipes and food suggestions that feature in this book.

CONTENTS

INTRODUCTION

The subject of weight loss and dieting inspires more fuss and nonsense than any other topic bar the Royal Family. Some of it is just daft – hands up who tried the Pineapple Diet? Some of it has been dangerous – notably the very low calorie diets that substituted a drink for proper food. A lot of it has been downright dishonest, particularly the diets that suggest you can eat all you want and still lose weight, or those that encourage you to pig out every so often. Many diets are difficult or time-consuming to put into practice, which is why we have problems following them for longer than a week or two. It is all very well for rich celebrities like Oprah Winfrey to trumpet their success in losing weight and then promote their methods and recipes for us to follow. But they have personal cooks who are paid to spend their time weighing the chicken breasts, skinning them, and thinking up some delicious, exciting way of serving them up to their employers on a bed of colour-coordinated, ribbon-cut vegetables in some exotic low-calorie sauce.

The way they describe and promote it, it all sounds wonderful and no doubt it is, if you can afford to have someone permanently slaving away in the kitchen. But most of us come home from work starving hungry each evening and just want to fix a satisfying meal quickly before we are tempted to raid the bread bin or biscuit tin.

In the real world complex rules and recipes with unconventional ingredients, however wonderful and delicious, invariably spell death to any sustained attempt at dieting. We then feel guilty because we have 'failed', preparing the ground, psychologically, for another attempt, and failure, in a few weeks' time.

This book is designed for people who want to lose weight and be slimmer on a permanent basis without resorting to extreme privation or having to follow a complex set of rules that involve them thinking about food – what to eat, what not to eat – for large sections of the day. You may just want to lose the five or six pounds that will take you down a dress size and let you wear a bikini with more confidence. You may know you need to lose a stone or two for health reasons as well as vanity. Reaching your target will obviously take you longer. Whatever your particular situation, you *can* lose the weight you want without becoming obsessive or a diet bore.

Indeed, the whole point of No Fuss Fat Loss is to make the process as simple, low-key, and therefore easy to stick to as possible, despite the huge amount of confusing and contradictory information that we are bombarded with constantly.

Huge amounts of money are spent promoting this or that wonder diet or slimming drug and producing 'research' designed to baffle us with science. There are scientific reports assuring us that overweight people really do not eat any more than slim people. On the other hand there are scientific

> *Most of us come home from work starving hungry and just want to fix a satisfying meal quickly before we are tempted to raid the biscuit tin*

> *Consuming more calories than you need results in weight gain*

reports showing the complete opposite. Slimming is particularly vulnerable to myths and fashionable obsessions. Once upon a time your metabolism was believed to be the crucial factor in overweight. Now diet gurus like to place the blame on allergies. As I write, wheat seems to have taken over from additives as food public enemy number one.

Naturally we all prefer to believe that being overweight and unfit can be blamed on something else outside our control. It is easy to sell someone the idea that they are a victim. But the truth is that your weight is entirely under your control. Weight loss boils down to a very simple concept: consuming more calories than you need results in weight gain; reducing calories and stepping up physical activity will result in weight loss. The bad news is that this takes effort. There is no quick fix for the seriously overweight. The good news is that this puts weight loss within everyone's grasp. For most of us it involves altering the balance and quantity of the food we eat and taking more exercise rather than slavishly counting calories. The tough news is that anyone who wants to achieve weight loss must be focused, determined, and honest about it if they want to succeed.

This book is designed to show you how to incorporate helpful weight-loss strategies into your everyday life and eating so that you achieve the weight loss you want – permanently.

CHAPTER ONE

Why We Put on Weight

AN UNNATURAL LIFESTYLE

Walk down any High Street and it will be perfectly obvious that many of us, of all ages, are overweight. It's not just the forty-plus men and women with 'middle-age spread'. There are plenty of jumbo-sized teenagers and children walking around, too.

It hasn't always been like this. Clothing manufacturers confirm that, in the post-war years, women have steadily got larger – Ms Average is reckoned to be a good two sizes bigger now than she was twenty-five years ago. Doctors and others in the health industry moan that obesity is fast becoming a major national disease. There is an upsurge in weight-related conditions like diabetes. Unfit children are an increasing concern in the school system. The UK is now following the appalling trend in the USA with some entrepreneurs opening fat farms for children.

This discernible and overall weight gain has not happened because our metabolism, on a national basis, has become lower or because more of us are genetically programmed to be tubby. If there is anything that demonstrates that weight is alterable and controllable, not something that is predetermined for us (or is due to allergies or some food ingredient), it is the fact that we are, on average, significantly plumper than we used to be. We must look for environmental causes.

The reasons are not hard to find. Basically, our continued weight gain is the entirely predictable result of changes in the way we live. It is the logical result of an increasingly unnatural lifestyle.

You do not see overweight animals in the wild. That is because they spend their day hunting for food – as did our caveman ancestors who used up most of their energy just surviving and providing for their immediate family. Getting enough to eat was hard work and the process was pretty active physically which kept intake in line with output. It provided a natural check on fatness.

> *Weight gain is the entirely predictable result of changes in the way we live. You do not see overweight animals in the wild*

We don't want to go back to a way of life where we spend the whole day looking for something to eat, but we do have to recognise the fundamental problem for what it is and realise that we have to do something about it. Overweight and obesity is a post-industrial problem. Somehow we have to compensate for the fact that daily life scarcely ever requires us to move a muscle.

THE CONSPIRACY OF EVERYDAY LIVING

Despite the fact that there has been a proliferation of health clubs, gyms, and various kinds of exercise and dance classes in the past few years, many of us are actually increasingly inactive in our everyday lives. It is a strange paradox. On the one hand, there are the keep-fit enthusiasts who make a big deal out of it all, often taking their leisure-time hobby to extremes. You have probably seen articles about fitness freaks who are addicted to their daily routine of workouts, which gives them a high, or who cannot stay away from the gym. On the other hand, there are those (and rather more of them) who do very little exercise at all. The fact is that we need to find a good balance in our physical activity in much the same way we need to find a good balance in our diet.

We spend too much time in our cars, or slumped on the sofa watching television. We spend too much time at work in our offices, too, which makes us too tired, we think, to take

> *We need to find a good balance in our physical activity in much the same way we need to find a good balance in our diet*

exercise when we get home. Ironically, as we have all become more health-conscious in some ways – drastically reducing our consumption of cigarettes for instance – everyday life increasingly conspires against our being as active as we should be for optimum fitness. Sure, more of us run the marathon these days and go to the gym, but it is also insidiously easy to slip into a completely sedentary lifestyle in which we have to make little or no physical effort for anything.

THE ROLE OF AGE

It gets worse as we get older and take on more commitments. Teenagers may not take formal exercise but they dance and party, which uses up a lot of energy, and they have to walk more to get from A to B – at least before they acquire a car. Mothers with young children, by contrast, may feel they are using up a lot of energy in the daily round of work, shopping, and the school run, but in reality are maybe getting little of the kind of exercise they need. In fact, lifting children and doing housework and shopping can be very damaging, since you are usually stressed at the time and not thinking about the strain that you are putting on different parts of the body or the way that you move. This kind of activity is exhausting, which is why so many women get out of the habit of taking the kind of exercise that energises them. There is all the difference between taking a brisk walk in the park and struggling the same distance through a crowded shopping precinct weighed down by shopping and toddlers.

Commuting workers feel much the same way. By the time they hit forty they are beginning to be less flexible – actually physically less able to do things. Most people do not realise how, as they get older, their reach and movements can become limited and restricted if they do not take regular exercise of some kind. The idea of exercise becomes unattractive and too much of an effort. It's a vicious circle.

THE ROLE OF PROCESSED FOOD

As it has become so much easier to be inactive, so it has become much, much easier for us to eat too much inappropriate food and distort our diets. So we are caught every which way. You could plot the steady trend in overweight over the past few decades against a graph of the growth of the processed food industry. That is not to demonise all the food industry's products, many of which we could not, and need not, do without. The idea of feeding a family without being able to fall back on a can or two of baked beans or a ready-made pizza when you wanted would be somewhat extreme. No doubt the purists and lentil-lovers would object but these products are perfectly sound, useful foods that few of us would like to be without. The point is that our daily diets can so easily become too dependent on them.

So, you may ask, what is the problem with that if pizza and beans are OK to eat?

It's not difficult to see why people get baffled and confused by food issues. Every now and again the newspapers will publish a report saying that fish and chips – the kind cooked in batter and oil and wrapped in newspaper – are a wonderful food. Doctors and nutritionists are quoted as pointing out that the traditional chip supper contains this, that, and the next vital ingredient, all of which are 'good' for you. Well, that may be true. Up to a point, almost *anything* that is presented to you to eat or that is available on the supermarket shelf contains *something* that is 'good' for you and nothing that, in normal circumstances, will cause you direct harm. On the other hand, it is just common sense that the nutrients to be found in fish and chips might be best enjoyed in some form that avoids eating all that batter and fat.

The real problem is that processed or prepared food tends to be heavily dependent on certain classes of ingredients – sugar, fat, and salt in particular. This makes them tasty and easy to eat, even somewhat addictive to the taste buds (and hence good business for the manufacturers), and they can end up displacing important foods like fruit and vegetables in our diet.

Manufacturers can be much more inventive with fat and sugar and salt; there is not an awful lot they can do with broccoli or mangoes, is there? There are not many ways in which they can 'add value' to them (thank goodness) or get people to overeat them (it takes too much time and effort). That is why you do not often see free samples of fruit and veg offered at the door of the supermarket by the ladies in white coats who always seem to be promoting yet another new variety of cheesy nibble. A huge amount of investment and inventiveness goes into producing these new products to tempt us with.

> *It is just so much easier to eat processed food*

Over the years, even those of us who regard ourselves as 'healthy' eaters are probably relying far too heavily on convenience or processed food, and the large number of calories they frequently contain, rather than taking fruit and vegetables as the starting blocks of our daily diet as did our caveman ancestors. Even our grandparents achieved a much better regime without really thinking about it, in the days before everyone had a car and a freezer full of processed food. What has changed over the last few decades as we have become fatter and fatter is the balance of our food intake. It has also had a knock-on effect on the overall amount that we eat, and therefore the number of calories we consume. It is just so much easier to eat processed food.

THE ROLE OF BLOOD SUGAR LEVELS

Food high in sugar is more quickly absorbed into our body's digestive system. One of the reasons why people love chocolate, for instance, is that eating it gives them an instant energy fix. Some chocoholics describe it as a high – a rush of good feeling that makes them feel energetic and on top of the world. It has been compared to taking a drug – or being in love.

What actually happens is that the chocolate, which is high in fat and sugar, causes a very swift rise in the body's blood sugar level, which makes you feel good. This is then followed by a rapid fall in blood sugar levels and you can start to feel tired, fed up and hungry again pretty quickly. You get irritable and look for another fix. Which is why some people are quite addicted to chocolate.

But the chocolate effect is probably only the most extreme and best-known example. The same underlying pattern applies in a less obvious way to much of the processed and convenience food on offer. You have probably noticed how, if you eat certain foods, you feel hungrier more quickly. It is easy to see how over-dependence on these foods – due to their availability and gratifying taste – results, over time, in a cycle of overeating and gradual weight gain.

By contrast, foods that are absorbed more slowly by the system – fruit and carbohydrates containing fibre, for instance, which takes time for the body to process – are believed to keep blood sugar levels more stable between meals, thereby helping to avoid hunger pangs and the desperate feeling that you want to binge. It is not necessary to go deeply into the biochemistry of all this; whole books have been written about what is known as the 'glycaemic response'

– the different rates at which various carbohydrate foods are absorbed and digested and the impact on our blood sugar. The point to remember is that overweight is linked to our increasing preference for refined and high-fat food, and that this is just one way in which the growth and popularity of processed food appears to have undermined our eating habits.

SPEED AND CONVENIENCE

It is not simply that it is easier to overeat convenience or processed food because they are physically easier and superficially more palatable to digest. A lot of us do not feel we have the time to do a lot of food preparation or cooking at home any more. A great deal of convenience or processed food promotion focuses on the busy executive or working mother (who is entitled to eschew the drudgery of the kitchen because she works so hard and is so successful). Much is made of the fact that families seldom eat together every day, and this is where all those individual convenience dishes stacked in the freezer come in so handy.

The reality, of course, is that it is just as quick and easy to concoct a simple and tasty stir-fry from a chicken breast and a bag of ready-cut supermarket veggies as it is to shove a convenience food in the oven or microwave. It takes very little more time to prepare some pasta and a tomato and herb sauce to go with it. The real truth is that for many of us, high-fat, high-salt, or high-sugar foods have become a habit. We have grown to prefer them, which is why the food manufacturers are now making a fortune selling us reduced-fat or reduced-calorie versions of the very same thing that helped make us fat in the first place.

> *For many of us, high-fat, high-salt or high-sugar foods have become a habit*

THE DINNER-PARTY SYNDROME

Part of the problem, paradoxically, is the way that we are currently being encouraged to take food and cooking more seriously. You can hardly turn on the television or open a newspaper or magazine without falling over someone discussing cooking or restaurants. Particular kinds of food, or ingredients, now seem to inspire a semi-religious fervour in their advocates as they go in and out of favour with baffling frequency. But despite all the hype and sales of cookery books, it does appear that more and more of us actually spend less and less time preparing and cooking food from scratch at home, preferring to concentrate our energies on producing something wonderful every so often for a dinner party. We seem to have convinced ourselves that preparing simple healthy satisfying meals in a low-key fashion is not a worthwhile pursuit any more. We feel that we are under pressure to produce something exciting and colourful, just as they do on television. The First World's attitude to food and eating is fast verging on the decadent – it's not so much what we eat as what it looks like.

THE BIG BANG METHOD

Most people try to lose weight by starting a strict diet on Day One and battling to stick to it. It is the Big Bang method of dieting. Suddenly, overnight, you are going to change the habits of a lifetime and be *really good this time*. This is almost certainly doomed to failure, particularly if you start on a severe exclusion diet of some kind. A diet like this is likely to spark off food cravings and make you feel deprived from the outset. It gives your body the message that it is physically starving, which often produces an urge to eat more than usual. Millions of dieters have found that they simply cannot stick to it and before long they are actually bingeing on the

> *Try to make some small changes and integrate them into your daily life*

forbidden foods as a result. So they end up eating much more than they would if they had not started a diet at all. This time do it differently, in a more low-key way. Just try to make some small changes and integrate them into your daily life.

BEFORE YOU START

Here are a few things to think about and do before you start a diet.

- Find some way to incorporate some extra exercise into your day. This should not be something that you have to organise yourself to do outside your normal routine but something that you can do most days. The easiest and most convenient exercise is probably walking – to the station or the bus, up a flight of stairs to the office instead of taking the lift – anything, so long as it gets you moving briskly for ten to twenty extra minutes a day. You will find that there are huge benefits in exercising. Not only will you help yourself get into better shape but you will feel both more alert mentally and more relaxed.
- Make an effort to avoid processed and convenience foods, and replace them with something else. Think ahead about what you are going to eat so that shopping for an evening meal doesn't become a rushed, frantic decision. Don't feel you have to produce anything exciting that is time-consuming and complicated. A salad, a risotto, or a stir-fry is nearly as fast to put together as most of the ready-prepared food on the supermarket shelves. And these dishes are much more delicious than anything that comes from a can or a packet.

- Make sure you eat at least three meals a day. Otherwise you will feel hungry and desperate. Contrary to what might be expected, many overweight people do not eat three meals a day, and many thin people eat more than three meals, preferring to eat smaller quantities of food more often. You will eventually find out what suits you best. But one thing is for sure: going without food for many hours a day will make losing weight harder in the long term, not easier. The *No Fuss Fat Loss* diet is not about making you feel deprived. It aims to help you lose weight by eating normally.

- Keep something delicious like a punnet of raspberries or strawberries around if you like to nibble while you are working or preparing meals. They are a good substitute for a chocolate bar or a quick slice of bread (see pages 78–9 as to why bread is not such a good idea). Have them ready, and don't think that you won't be tempted – you will be. These kind of fruit 'treats' are low calorie, nutritionally good for you, and taste lovely. You will not feel deprived and that will help you stick to your food plan. Face the fact that you are not going to lose weight if you indulge in cakes, puddings, pastries, and biscuits. Substitute fruit for dessert.

- Make a conscious effort to eat more fruit and vegetables. The health benefits are well known. The current thinking is that you should eat a *minimum* of five helpings a day and many of us don't even manage that on a regular basis.

- Get into the habit of drinking plenty of water, even if you don't feel particularly thirsty. Keep a bottle of water near you at work as well as at home. Water can help you feel less hungry. Water also 'oils' the system and helps combat constipation (see below), which is exacerbated (and sometimes caused) by not drinking enough water.

Constipation is usually due to a combination of factors. Apart from lack of water, a diet low in fibre and too little exercise are two of the other major culprits, both of which can also

make you overweight. So it is not surprising that overweight people may also find themselves constipated much of the time.

Tips

- High-fibre foods like vegetables and fruit hold water, which creates bulk and softens the stools. You often hear about the need for the fibre but in fact the fibre needs sufficient water to be effective.

- Exercise is also important since it helps the bowel stay fit and effective. When you run, for instance, you are toning up the muscles of your internal organs as well as improving the shape of your hips and thighs.

CHAPTER TWO

Why We Find it so Hard to Lose Weight

THE NO-FAT OBSESSION

Anyone who visits the USA usually notices two things: it seems to have a higher proportion of truly obese people than anywhere else in the world; and, at the same time, the US is the most diet- and weight-obsessed nation on the planet. Walk around any American supermarket and you will notice how the shelves groan with low-calorie this and low-fat or fatless that. At the bakery counter, you will routinely see no-fat muffins and other no-fat versions of delicious-looking cakes and biscuits lined up with the other offerings in a way that does not happen in the UK – yet. Hopefully it never will. Judging from the American experience, the more weight- and calorie-conscious (or obsessive) people are, the harder it seems to be for them to lose weight. Offering no-fat carrot cake (it may be no-fat but there is probably loads of sugar in it) actually helps you to get fatter since it encourages you to eat the kind of food you should simply say no to if you have really made up your mind to lose weight.

THE DIET INDUSTRY

But inability to resist a gooey cake is only part of the reason why many of us find it so hard to lose weight. The main reason is that the diet industry has encouraged people to seek a quick fix, promising the loss of so many pounds in a week, the answer to a lifetime's

The standard reaction to a decision to lose weight is to embark on a crash diet and eat hardly anything at all

excess in days. Even if you do not actually try one of the diets that promise to get you looking good in your bikini within a few days, the standard reaction to a decision to lose weight is to embark on a crash diet and eat hardly anything at all.

THE YO-YO PATTERN

Many women start doing this in adolescence, semi-starving themselves on and off at various times over the years with limited success. What they don't realise is that the body becomes used to this yo-yo pattern of dieting. It adapts to it, which means that crash diets become less and less effective at shifting a few pounds just when you want them to. Moreover, a quickie diet is not the best way to get rid of fat. The weight loss experienced as the result of a crash diet is due to the body losing the water that surrounds the fat cells.

CRASH DIETS

Several scientific reviews have looked at the 'quality' of weight loss under various diet regimes – measuring the amount of fat (as opposed to muscle or water) actually lost. The bottom line of this research is that the weight loss achieved by quickie crash diets is often due to loss of water and muscle rather than fat. These 'crash diets' are quite different from a food and exercise plan designed to gradually shift the body's fat and improve muscle tone. Worse, when you start to eat normally after a crash diet, the weight piles on very fast. This has been the experience of many women who went on the very low calorie diets that became popular in the 1980s.

There is plenty of scientific evidence to show that, faced with what it assumes is imminent starvation, the body has the capacity to store fat to get ready for tough times ahead. That is why, when you start eating normally after being on a diet, you can find yourself putting on an alarming amount of weight very quickly. It seems to be the way that the body is programmed to deal with the food shortages our ancestors often experienced. The other explanation for increased weight gain after one of these diets is that the loss of muscle encourages the body to burn calories less efficiently, storing more as fat. (The higher the proportion of muscle a person has, the more calories are required for basic functions.)

HORMONES AND THE URGE TO BINGE

Many women blame their hormones, or their age, for the increased difficulty they have in losing weight as they get older. Age probably plays a part because we tend to be less active the older we are, but the body's resistance to a lifetime of crash dieting is probably a big factor, too.

It is not just this physical reaction that makes it hard to lose weight. The conventional diet culture affects us psychologically as well. The most common problem is that, having started out on a ridiculously difficult diet regime (less than 800 calories a day is considered a very low calorie regime; the liquid food substitute diets you may see advertised aim for 400–600 calories a day), we pretty quickly fall below the ludicrously tough standards we have set ourselves and actually start eating anything and everything. We feel we can always start again tomorrow, so we had better eat today all the gorgeous things we are going to have to give up tomorrow.

There are many theories about why that happens – why we get the urge to binge. The charitable theory, assiduously peddled by most diet books, is that our bodies crave certain nutrients and that we just cannot control the urge to scoff everything in sight as a result. Amazingly, all this stuff that our bodies feel in need of is contained in chocolate and cakes and lovely crusty bread. We don't seem to have the same uncontrollable urge for steamed fish or lettuce, do we?

In truth, most bouts of binge eating (which, at the extreme, can be a sign of serious mental illness) are probably due as much to the frailties of human nature and good old fashioned greed as to any need for essential nutrients. Our relationship with food has been so distorted by commercial pressures that many of us can't think straight about it any more. We use food to comfort ourselves. We use food to calm ourselves down. We use food to liven ourselves up if we are tired and stressed. If we have tried and failed to stick to a diet that is too ambitious, then eating all the forbidden foods is one perfectly normal and understandable reaction to our frustration and disappointment. Some diets promise that you can pig out every now and again as some kind of reward for succeeding with the rest of the diet. This is just a formalisation of the bingeing instinct that bedevils so many attempts to lose weight. It is also one reason why it is very important to eat at least three meals a day and not allow yourself to become desperately hungry. If you feel constantly hungry, you will probably end up eating more than if you were not on a diet at all.

YOUR RELATIONSHIP TO FOOD

The conclusion that this is leading to is that dieting can be self-defeating because it leads to an obsession with food. Understanding and taking on board a few simple principles about food and your relationship to it is much more helpful for weight loss than any amount of fussy calorie counting or exclusion. Losing weight is not easy and no one should pretend it is.

> *Dieting can be self-defeating because it leads to an obsession with food*

Slim people spend their lives hearing how overweight people hardly eat a thing, really. They are overweight because they have a slow metabolism, or a tendency to cellulite, or they have a food allergy of some kind. Whilst a growing number of women do seem to put on weight because of thyroid problems (if you have gained a noticeable amount of extra weight over a couple of months for no apparent reason, you should have your thyroid checked by your doctor before embarking on a diet), overweight is, in the vast majority of cases, due to individual lifestyle factors rather than things over which you have no control. That is the tough truth. Unfortunately excuses – most of them so much pseudo-scientific hocus-pocus peddled by therapists who make as much money out of us as the fast food manufacturers – are as readily available in our everyday life as the food that is basically responsible for our overweight.

FEMINIST THEORIES

Perhaps the biggest amount of unhelpful codswallop has come from the feminists who argue that women's desire to lose weight and get into a more attractive shape is really part of a conformist tyranny foisted on them by men, with the help of the fashion industry, which, by insisting on showing waif-like models with freak proportions, exploits women's insecurities. These theories, and the accompanying therapy sessions they generate, have probably made nearly as much money for their proponents as the batty diets involving eating six pineapples

> *Just because we have let the weight creep up over the years does not make it 'natural'*

a day or three Mars Bars – and are not nearly so funny or enjoyable.

All this takes our concentration away from the central hard facts. Many of us *are* overweight. It is not something that we have been brainwashed into thinking, it is a fact. It is also a fact that a good two thirds of us would be immensely improved not just in looks but more importantly in health by losing half a stone right now. Just because we have let the weight creep up over the years does not make it 'natural', as militant heavyweight feminists would have us believe. Far from it.

You have to be determined about losing weight if you are going to succeed. Being slimmer and fitter is something you do for yourself. It has absolutely nothing to do with sexual politics or stereotyping. It applies just as much to overweight men of all ages.

THE ROLE OF GENES

People also become confused by the part played by genes in their shape and weight. They can become fatalistic, believing that overweight is inherited and that they must inevitably follow the pattern of their parents or other members of the family. There has been substantial scientific research on the impact of genes versus environment which seems to suggest that, whilst body shape and a tendency to overweight can be inherited, what you yourself actually do in the way of diet and exercise has just as much bearing on body weight.

THE ROLE OF THE WESTERN DIET

Recent statistics from the diagnostics company Medisys indicate how just a decade or two of Western-style eating has

caused obesity and other health problems in men and women of Eastern cultures – notably the Japanese and the Chinese – where they had previously been rare. This points to the commonsense conclusion that how you yourself live and behave is probably more important than any tendencies you feel you have inherited. One generation of hamburger eating has put a dent in the Japanese health statistics, which now show a swiftly rising incidence of diseases associated with a Western diet. Their traditional fare, rich in soya (a phyto-oestrogen that research has shown reduces the body's exposure to the hormones that cause breast and testicular cancer) and based on fish and vegetables, seemed to protect them against some diseases.

In the West scientific tests are in progress to determine the impact of these phyto-oestrogens in the prevention of certain cancers – and one group of British scientists has backed the launch of a health bar containing these substances. (The Tenovus research centre in Wales has been reviewing the role of phyto-oestrogens and diet in the international incidence of breast and prostate cancers, and has put together a great deal of evidence that points to diet being a central issue.)

A change of diet seems to change the experience of Eastern cultures very quickly. Medical supply companies are even now anticipating that China will become a huge new market for blood glucose-measuring products because the change to a Western diet is expected to result in a huge increase in the rate of diabetes among the population. Environment and habits are just as important as genetic inheritance. The food you eat is crucial. Your weight is in your hands.

THE ROLE OF METABOLISM

Many people blame their excess weight on a metabolism that takes longer to burn off consumed calories. Like everything else, your metabolism may be to some extent genetically determined but it is by no means clear that the descriptions 'slow' or 'fast' mean very much in terms of the difference between various individuals' natural metabolic rate. Ironically, if you starve yourself, or are inactive, your metabolic rate will be lower than if you eat properly and take a decent amount of exercise. So this is something at least partially within your control and it is easily achieved.

One reason why metabolism has become one of the perennial excuses for overweight is that drugs that stimulate the metabolism are known to be a quick way of losing weight. It should be pointed out that using drugs in this way is a health hazard, though there have always been doctors who will prescribe them to models and others desperate to lose a few

> *If you starve yourself, or are inactive, your metabolic rate will be lower than if you eat properly and take a decent amount of exercise*

pounds in a hurry. And the fact that weight can be lost through stimulating the metabolism artificially does not mean that your normal metabolism is to blame for your excess pounds.

THE MYTH OF CELLULITE

One of the biggest myths is that cellulite is a different kind of fat afflicting women through no fault of their own. What is commonly known as cellulite, which is supposed to form mainly around the thighs and hips, has spawned an entire industry, with books and detox diets and hugely expensive fat-dispersing creams available at a beauty or health counter near you. Cellulite is often said to be a harder fat, more difficult to break down and get rid of than, say, fat on your stomach or waist. French scientists and dermatologists believe passion-ately in cellulite, as well they might since they are generously paid by a hugely economically important beauty industry. But the theories expounded about cellulite make most of their UK counterparts laugh themselves silly. Cellulite, they prefer to believe, is just another word for fat and only diet and exercise will help. This theory, of course, does not sell quite so many bottles and tubes, the true benefits of which will be apparent to anyone who has tried them. All that massaging is pretty good for the skin and seems to improve the look and feel of your limbs on a temporary basis, but the only answer to permanently losing weight or, if you prefer, cellulite, is diet and exercise.

DIETING AS DENIAL

Perhaps the biggest problem is persevering with a weight-loss regime once you start. We have all been programmed to see dieting as denial, as not being allowed to eat what we like when we like. Even talking about 'a diet' is unhelpful because it is so often linked to previous failure. What we are actually aiming for is to find a way of eating normally that will help us shed excess pounds and stop them piling back on again. So

> *The biggest problem is persevering with a weight-loss regime once you start*

don't think of this as 'going on a diet' or giving things up. Think about it as eating healthily and well.

Behind the feelings of denial there is the underlying idea that somehow we are really *entitled* to eat too many basically useless, unnecessary and unhealthy things – and the implication is that one day we will be able to eat like that again. However, it is impossible to lose weight on a permanent basis unless we are prepared to make a permanent adjustment to the habits that made us overweight in the first place. Sorry, but that's the truth.

WOMEN AND FOOD

The problem is that many of us, women in particular, have an irrational and immature approach to food. It probably starts sometime in childhood: if food from a parent becomes a reward, or if you were always told to finish the food on your plate regardless of whether or not you were full, or if you saw food as a treat ('naughty but nice' ran the advertisement for fresh cream cakes a few years ago). All kinds of emotional issues arise around food – feelings of guilt and the need for comfort, for instance, or the feeling that you deserve to be able to eat this or that. So it comes to represent something far removed from what it is: the basic stuff that keeps the body going and is enjoyable to prepare and eat.

TEENAGERS AND FOOD

Teenage girls become confused by the battery of contradic-tory health and slimming messages beamed at them through the media. Their mothers in turn become terrified of discussing food and weight issues in case the girls end up getting anorexia nervosa, the 'slimming disease', that can result in long-term damage and even death. But those of us who are brought up to think about food and exercise as important to life in a sensible, positive way, are far less likely to succumb to eating disorders. That good old British tradition which holds that there is something a little wrong in caring too much about your appearance is probably partly responsible for the recent epidemic of anorexia nervosa, since it is obvious to any intelligent girl that appearance *does* matter a great deal, even if her parents insist on telling her differently and will she please just concentrate on those A-level grades.

MEN AND FOOD

Throughout their adult lives, many women find food a highly emotional issue and this makes it psychologically very hard for them to stay on a diet. Some indication of this can be seen by observing men who manage to diet successfully. They are often much more straightforward about it, sticking to a diet and achieving weight loss as a result. Food doesn't appear to be an emotional issue with them in the way that it is with many women, although there does seem to be a growing number of young men with anorexia, too.

MEDIA PRESSURE

One reason for this may be that young men as well as women are starting to feel pressurised by the continual stream of images of 'ideal' beauty in newspapers and magazines. With all these images around, it is all too easy to decide that you are never going to look like Kate Moss or Brad Pitt anyway, and just give up trying to lose weight. It is important to be realistic about your shape and body weight. No diet in the world is going to make you grow long legs, but a leaner, fitter body, whatever your basic shape, will always look more attractive than an unfit, overweight one and, more importantly, will make you feel both physically better and better about yourself.

NO FUSS

Many diets don't work because calorie counting individual foods and portions is fiddly and irritating to anyone else living within range of you. There are plenty of half-hearted dieters who worry aloud over menus in restaurants and who block up supermarket aisles reading the labels on tins to make sure that they avoid this and that substance. This is not living; it is not surprising that so many people are quickly bored by trying to lose weight if that is what is believed to be necessary for success.

One important aspect of the No Fuss Fat Loss system is that you concentrate on what you can and must eat every day to feel well and healthy. No one needs to become obsessive in order to eat properly, although many faddy diets seem to operate on the principle that time-consuming fuss might give the slimming victim something to do and think about to take their mind off the missing goodies.

ONE LAST THOUGHT

Everyone can be a sucker for the quick fix approach and we love the idea (promoted by newspaper headlines with monotonous regularity) that we can eat all we want and still lose weight. The fact is that every single diet ever devised has revolved around calorie reduction and eating less, even if that has not been the stated aim, the selling point. We have been bombarded with low-fat diets and high-fat diets, low-carbohydrate diets and high-carbohydrate diets, all-protein diets, food-combining diets, and food-exclusion diets. One way or the other they are all about limiting calories. Each method has its own high priest or priestess who damns or eulogises particular foods with evangelical fervour, bringing in swathes of scientific evidence to support their particular theory. The various elements and substances contained in all our basic foodstuffs

Every single diet ever devised has revolved around calorie reduction and eating less

become personalities in their own right as we are encouraged to imagine them scurrying around inside our bodies doing good or evil. *No Fuss Fat Loss* does not pretend that it is easy to lose weight. But a sensible straightforward approach to losing weight by restoring a proper balance to the food you eat is the one that is going to work, permanently.

CHAPTER THREE

What You Eat

WHAT DO YOU EAT?

The first thing is to establish exactly what you do eat over a period of three or four days. That should be long enough to establish the truth, and it is helpful if the period you look at takes in at least part of a weekend, since sometimes our diet is different then from on work days. It helps to write down everything you eat in that time, just to give yourself an idea of where you may be going wrong. Doctors often recommend that you should complete a week's or a fortnight's food diary, but if you are sensible and honest with yourself a few days is really all that is required.

WHAT IS THE RIGHT DIET?

There is no particularly 'right' diet for everyone. How can there be when we all have such different lifestyles? An athlete will need a very different diet from an office worker. However, medical science has given us some broad guidelines on what does and does not constitute a proper *balanced* diet, and it is useful to compare our own to this standard. Roughly speaking, a healthy diet would have a third of the calorie intake in the form of fruit or vegetables and a third in the form of starches like bread, pulses, and pasta. The remaining third would be in the form of dairy product-based food, plus meat and fish. Note that the last list is one category – one third – for all those things. Broadly

There is no particularly 'right' diet for everyone

BREAKFAST Approx Calories		MID AFTERNOON SNACK	
2 slices toast, butter and marmalade	400	tea, milk and sugar	50
coffee, milk and sugar	50	slice of shortbread	145
low fat yoghurt	150	EVENING	
MID MORNING SNACK		bag of crisps	130
coffee, milk and sugar	50	1/2 beer	284
2 digestive biscuits	140	pork chop	275
		roast potatoes	145
LUNCH		broccoli	14
Slice of pizza	400	apple tart	250
tomato salad	30	cream	200
french dressing	100		
ice-cream	200	TOTAL CALORIES	3013

speaking, most doctors and nutritionists would regard this pattern as sensible and healthy.

It is important that diets are, within those categories, as varied as possible. That way, we can be sure of getting all the nutrients we need to keep ourselves healthy. We get protein, the building block of the body that forms all our cells and organs, from meat, fish, nuts, and dairy products such as milk and cheese. One major feature of the Western diet is the high quantity of protein we consume. We have been programmed to believe that protein is 'good' (in the way that 'fat' means bad). And protein *is* good, but we probably eat too much of it. Carbohydrates, which include fruit and vegetables as well as starchy foods like bread and pasta, are a major source of energy and fibre.

WHAT ABOUT FAT?

Although fat is generally regarded as bad for you, your body actually needs some kinds of fats to work efficiently and well. Fish oil and olive oil are two examples of fats that contain nutrients known as essential fatty acids. The body cannot manufacture these itself so we need to eat them. Some of these essential fatty acids are believed to protect against heart attacks, strokes, and even some cancers and they all have a vital role in cell metabolism.

Your body actually needs some kinds of fats to work efficiently

MAKING CHOICES

All the major food groups contain some of the vitamins and other nutrients that we need, so we must include all of them in our diets. Within those different food groups there are some serious choices to be made, since we are aiming to get optimum nutrition and eating satisfaction at the lowest calorie 'cost'. For instance, there is protein in red meat – but along with the protein comes a high level of saturated fat. You can avoid it by eating fish or game, which contains far less fat but just as much protein.

Another example of food choice is bread. There is a big nutritional difference between the flabby, ready-sliced white loaf wrapped in plastic and a good wholemeal bread. Although both are starchy carbohydrates, wholemeal bread has over twice, sometimes as much as three times, the fibre of white bread, which transforms its nutritional role.

It comes back to the question raised earlier: is traditional battered fish and chips 'good' for you? We need to eat some items from all the food groups every day, but for optimum nutrition and health we have to pay attention to our individual choices within them, particularly if we want to lose weight.

So let's compare this very rough guide to what constitutes a sensible diet with what you actually eat.

THE HARSH TRUTH

Prepare yourself for a shock. Most of us like to think that we eat healthily, which is one reason why we get so frustrated when we put on weight and cannot lose it. We feel that we don't deserve to be overweight because we really do not eat too badly. But the harsh truth is that when confronted with the evidence of a food diary, most of us realise that we don't have nearly such a healthy diet as we think we have.

Despite some improvement in the content of our diet the statistics collected by the Government demonstrate that fat still makes up too high a proportion of our diets. In the UK, for instance, the latest figures available (1997 National Food Survey) show that fat makes up an average 39.2 per cent of our food intake, and within that, saturated fat makes up the biggest single category at over 15 per cent. The Government goal is to reduce total fat intake to less than 35 per cent over the next five years.

ARE YOU EATING HIDDEN FAT?

Eating too much high-fat food is the major culprit in many individual cases of overweight. You may think that this does not apply to you and it may not, but it is only when you go through your food diary that it will become clear how much hidden fat (not to mention sugar) you may actually be eating in the course of a normal day.

Bear in mind that, weight for weight, fat contains more than double the calories of carbohydrate and protein.

You might start the day with toast for **breakfast**. Nothing particularly bizarre about that. But if you spread your toast with butter or margarine, you are doing two things: first, you are probably doubling the amount of calories you are eating; and second, you are probably taking nearly half the calories you eat for your first meal of the day in the form of fat.

> *Eating too much high-fat food is the major culprit in many individual cases of overweight*

Let's move on to **lunch**. Perhaps you have a slice of quiche and a green salad with some dressing. You might think this is fairly healthy. However, depending on the amount you eat, the chances are that some two thirds of the calories in this high-calorie meal come from fat, since quiche, particularly commercially produced quiche, has a high fat content. Just think of the ingredients: eggs, cheese, flour, and baking fats.

Now for **supper**. You choose something simple like lamb chops with vegetables and rice or potatoes – all normal healthy food. It may well give you a much better-balanced individual meal, provided you trim the fat off the chops, but the fact of the matter is that when you analyse what you have eaten that day, you are probably fair and square in the category of people with an unhealthily high-fat diet. You have not eaten any junk food, cream cakes, chocolates, puddings, or chips – none of the great no-noes of eating. You have not over-indulged. You may even feel you have not eaten very much at all. But it is clear that your diet is not as balanced as it should be. Two thirds of your total intake is in the protein, meat, and dairy products category, much of which is high in fat. You have probably eaten far less in the way of the fruit and vegetables or the starches and cereals that should each make up one third of your total diet than is healthy. It isn't necessary to count calories or read labels obsessively to work out pretty quickly whether or not you have a diet that is over-dependent on this one category of foods, which should really account for only a third of your total diet.

ASSESS YOUR FAT INTAKE

Taking your three- or four-day food diary, go through each day making a rough assessment of the proportion of high-fat food you have in your everyday diet. You may get a surprise. Add in any puddings, after-dinner cheese, chocolate bars, or snacks and crisps you may have along the way, and what you think is your healthy, not-so-high-fat diet begins to look more like a cause for concern. But you are not unusual.

If you rely on convenience or processed food for some of your meals, you may be sure that much of it will fall into a high-fat category. Processed food also contains a surprising amount of sugar – and not just in the obvious items like biscuits and cakes. Sugar is used routinely in items like baked beans and a whole range of other foods that we think of as savoury rather than sweet.

AN UNBALANCED DIET

Even if you prepare all your own meals yourself, it is easy to follow a diet that is not properly balanced, day after day, week after week, without realising it. The trouble is that many higher-fat proteins such as cheese, eggs, and meat are very easy to prepare and eat in a hurry. One of the things that has gone wrong with our attitude to food is that we assume that the mere avoidance of processed or junk food means that we are eating 'properly'. Unfortunately, given the way our food and cuisine has evolved, few of us can achieve the right balance in our diet without giving the matter some thought. It is far too easy to make high-fat proteins the cornerstone of

A food diary can help you identify the inessential intake that you should cut back on if you want to lose weight

most meals. That is where the majority of us go wrong and it is one of the major reasons why we put on weight.

Keeping a food diary for a few days may pinpoint other problems, too. What you may think of as just the occasional glass of wine or beer may add up to quite a lot. You may be surprised at the amount of snacks or crisps you eat. A food diary can help you identify the inessential intake that you should cut back on if you want to lose weight.

WHAT SHOULD YOU EAT?

But don't just think in terms of restrictions. Crucially, you must also look at what you are *not* eating – or not eating enough of. The chances are that there are significant nutritional gaps in your normal eating pattern. Most doctors and nutritionists agree that eating *at least* five helpings a day of fresh fruit or vegetables is important. As I pointed out earlier, many nutritionists would say that a really good diet would contain anything up to *double* that quantity.

Ten helpings is actually a pretty vast amount. To visualise it, think of a small apple or orange or a spoonful of carrots as one helping. Yes, it's ten of those – although, of course, you should spread your intake over a wider variety of fruit and vegetables. If you prefer, you can go by weight. Five servings is reckoned to be a total of 400 grams, so ten servings is equivalent to 800 grams. To put that in perspective, a medium-sized carrot is 100 grams.

Fruit and vegetables are pretty filling. This highlights one obvious and simple way that your diet can be improved. If you make a determined effort to include more fruit and vegetables, you will have to substitute them for the things you eat too much of at present. The benefits of this are not just that your diet would then conform more closely to what the nutritionists and other experts broadly agree is healthy. (The current Government target, for instance, is to increase average

> **If you make a determined effort to include more fruit and vegetables, you will have to substitute them for the things you eat too much of at present**

consumption of fruit and vegetables by 50 per cent in the interests of promoting health.) You will also find that it leads to an automatic reduction in the amount of calories you consume.

Tips to top up fruit and veg intake

- Start your evening meal with a first course of vegetable crudités or munch them as you prepare the meal. A sliced, medium-sized carrot and courgette, for instance, equal a couple of vegetable helpings.
- Keep fruit nibbles to hand – strawberries, raspberries, blueberries, kiwi fruit, mandarins, and fresh apricots are all tasty. Use these to stave off hunger pangs rather than having biscuits or a slice of bread.

FOOD IS NOT THE ENEMY

Getting balance back into your normal diet is one of the most valuable things you can do to help yourself lose weight. It might also help you manage your appetite better, too. One of the saddest things that happens when people start trying to cut down on an arbitrary basis is that food becomes the enemy. But without satisfying, regular meals, we become hungry, irritable, and unwell – and soon give up the idea of dieting. Our bodies need food. Food is wonderful – whether it is some beautiful, complex dish prepared in a top restaurant or a gorgeously ripe plum straight from the tree in your own garden. To regard it as 'the enemy' is a dreadful distortion – quite obscene when you consider the number of people in the world who truly go hungry and suffer from malnutrition.

Artificial starvation – dieting, in other words – is calculated to set up the cravings that lead to bingeing and make it impossible to follow any sensible, rational eating plan.

RESTORING THE BALANCE

Restoring the balance of your food helps you focus instead on what you *can* and *should* eat to achieve a healthy diet. Eating three meals a day means that you should not be hungry, and getting the balance right means that your body will not feel that it is being deprived. The easiest way of doing this without constantly referring to calorie counters or worrying about what you can eat is to divide your daily intake between the three categories of food, making each of them the central focus for one meal. That means that you will make sure that you eat all the things you should *each day* and stop depending too much on the protein group which includes most fats.

Many diet plans involve dividing calories between daily meals and snacks. This is irritating and time-consuming. It is also very hard to know what the correct number of calories should be for each individual portion, meal, or person. There are so many variables. How active are you? What is your size? What is your age? It is very difficult to pinpoint the exact number of calories you should restrict yourself to each day in order to lose weight. Long term, it is not the answer to the problem because it does not ensure that you eat healthily and in a way that allows you to *maintain* your weight loss once you have achieved it.

> *Eating three meals a day means that you should not be hungry*

FINDING THE RIGHT PATTERN

By dividing your food intake into kinds of food, you can also find the pattern that suits you best. Many people believe that you should 'breakfast like a king, lunch like a prince and dine in the evening like a pauper'. The theory is that you 'work off' breakfast and lunch during the day whereas a heavy meal at night causes you to put on weight. Nothing has been proved scientifically on that front, but you might find some eating patterns more comfortable and easier to live with than others. For instance, some people find that a really filling carbohydrate- or protein-based breakfast sets them up for the day and that they don't feel really hungry again until the evening. Others find that eating a substantial breakfast results in their feeling very hungry by lunchtime.

EATING TOO MUCH

You may also need to cut down on the overall amount of food you eat if you are trying to lose weight. There is no doubt that, just as we often rely too much on certain types of food, we can also quickly get into the habit of simply eating too much – particularly when what is on offer is so tempting. In most cases, however, getting the balance of food right is the solution to weight loss. We rarely overdose on fruit and vegetables; it is much more likely that we eat too much of the more calorific protein or starchy foods. Keep a firm check on this and the weight should come off. If it doesn't, you should investigate what else might be wrong – a thyroid imbalance, for instance.

Eat less, live longer

Interestingly, scientists now believe that people who have a nutritious but essentially sparse and calorie-restricted diet tend to live longer than their well-fed (in volume terms) contemporaries. Cutting down on the amount you eat (provided you eat well in terms of quality) may well be one way to improve your chances of a healthier old age. Fascinatingly, the population of Georgia, which has the lowest average intake of fat in the whole of Europe (16 per cent), is believed to have some of the most long-lived citizens in the world.

When you compile your food diary you may think that the balance of your food is not so different from that suggested by nutritionists and doctors. If you are overweight you may simply be eating too much – even though the proportions of any one of your meals, or your diet as a whole, do not seem far off the recommended amounts.

GOOD HABITS

As you gear up to embarking on your diet there are a number of good habit-forming strategies that should help you.

Try to eat only when you are hungry

Whilst it is self-defeating to deliberately starve yourself, it is a fact that food is immensely more enjoyable when you have worked up a good appetite. If you try to time your meals only for when you feel hungry, you will quickly reach the stage where it feels quite uncomfortable and inappropriate to eat unless you really need to.

Don't eat your food too quickly

Take time to enjoy it and chew everything thoroughly. It takes time for your body to register that it has had enough food for the moment, thank you. Some people eat so fast that they inevitably end up eating more than they need because the sensory message has not had the time to get through to the brain. Eating too fast makes it easier to eat too much.

> *Some people eat so fast that they inevitably end up eating more than they need*

Never have second helpings
Don't feel guilty about having food left over when you have finished a meal. Throw it away rather than keep it in the fridge, and if you think this is an awful waste, you will be encouraged to make less of it next time. What are you saving it for? And remember, if you are feeding children at different times from your own main meal, don't finish up their food.

Analyse your grazing habits
When you are tempted to eat when you are not hungry or indulge in something you really should not – chocolate or a slice of gooey cake – try to analyse what the big attraction is. Why and when do you do it? Are you bored and just want some kind of stimulation? Are you excited and happy about something? Have you had a setback or do you suddenly feel depressed? Does it happen at a particular time of day? You have to break the connection between your emotions and your food habits. That takes some will-power and determination but it is a vital factor in helping you lose weight and keeping it off in the future. In many cases it is this kind of aimless grazing that causes slow, steady weight gain over the years. It may be all that stands between you and a slimmer shape.

Adopt the two-starter regime
If you have to go out to business lunches and dinners where you will be expected to have two or more courses, don't treat it as an excuse either to abandon your diet or to create a fuss about having to stick to one. Ordering two starters, rather than a starter and a main course, is perfectly acceptable and will not make anyone else feel awkward or even arouse any comment.

Shop more often
Try to shop more often for smaller amounts of food – ideally a day or two's worth at a time. That means you will not buy more

than you have planned to prepare and it cuts down the temptation to make impulse buys while you are wheeling a giant shopping trolley round the supermarket feeling like an earth mother. If you shop daily

Try to shop more often for smaller amounts of food

with a hand basket, you can usually whizz through the fast till in the supermarket and you simply will not want to lug around more food that you need to.

A WAY OF EATING

The main thing to grasp is that this way of eating is not a diet, with all the restrictions and deprivations it implies. Yes, there are some things that you must avoid if you want to lose weight – that is only common sense. But this eating plan means that you eat healthily and normally, three times a day. And it is a No Fuss pattern that you can follow comfortably without even thinking about it, which will enable you to keep the weight off for ever.

CHAPTER FOUR

Fat Facts

LIFE'S TOO SHORT TO COUNT CALORIES

Cutting down on the fat content in our food is the most effective way to radically reduce the number of calories we consume. This is because, weight for weight, fat contains more calories than carbohydrates (including sugar), or protein. We know that we have to reduce calories, but the *No Fuss* approach means that we won't be permanently counting them and boring ourselves and everyone else.

Targeting the high-fat food that we eat is the first thing to do when adjusting our diets. You may have to spend a bit of time at first thinking about substitutions and alternatives and how to prepare food in a slightly different way, but it will quickly become second nature. It is important to understand that cutting back on fat is designed to restore your daily diet to a regime that is balanced and healthy. What I am proposing is very different from the very low fat or no-fat diets that have been popular over the last few years.

LOW-FAT DIETS

The theory behind many of these other diets is as follows. A very low fat regime does not just reduce calories and help you lose weight. It is supposed to shift the excess fat on your body in a kind of spot reduction without exercise, which means that if you need to lose fat from your thighs or tummy, that is where you will lose the vital inches. This has never been medically or

A no-fat or very low-fat diet is pretty boring and miserable to follow

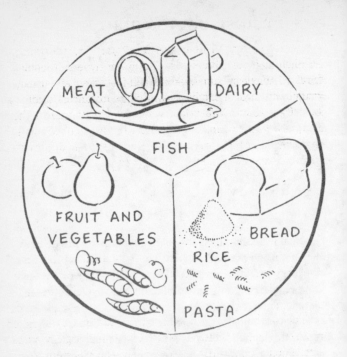

scientifically proven to work, although thousands of keen followers claim that it does and it has made fortunes for its promoters. That way of dieting is no- or low-fat but it does not really add up to a very attractive way of eating.

The main practical problem is that a no-fat or very low fat diet is pretty boring and miserable to follow and is certainly not something you want to do for any length of time, which means that if you simply go back to your old way of eating, you will start to put on weight again, which is no good. The whole purpose of the No Fuss approach is that you must find a way of eating that you enjoy, while helping yourself lose weight.

DEMONISING FOOD

It is never correct to demonise a natural food substance, although many diet books do. The no-fat hype surrounding food in American supermarkets (no-fat cakes are usually loaded with sugar and dubious synthetic substances) is ridiculous. If you want to lose weight, why are you eating cake in the first place? Many people regard sugary foods as public enemy number one, and of course these kinds of foods do usually contain a lot of fat as well.

MODERN EATING

As I've already said, weight for weight, fat contains more than double the calories of carbohydrate and protein, which underlines the whole problem of modern eating and weight loss. The improvement in Western standards of living (not the same thing as quality of life) has resulted in the individual consumption of increased amounts of fat over the last few decades, although consumption is now on a downward trend. Our diets are over-reliant on proteins in the form of meat or dairy products, and the increased availability of protein in Western countries has been matched by increased height as well as girth in successive generations. The real villain, however, is the easy availability of luxuries – cakes, puddings, snacks, chocolate products, and other processed foods – which, because they contain a lot of fat, have disrupted the balance of our diets.

The basic fact is that you will put on weight if you take in more calories than you use up in energy – and you will lose weight if you consume less than your body uses. Reducing the

The real villain is the easy availability of luxuries – cakes, puddings, snacks, chocolate products, and other processed foods

amount of fat is the quickest way to reduce calories.

HIGH-FAT FOODS

One gram of fat is equivalent to nine calories, while the same weight of protein or carbohydrate is equivalent to four calories. High-fat foods, then, are more calorific than high-protein or high-carbohydrate foods. That means, roughly, that a skinless chicken breast or salmon fillet, for instance, will contain less than half the calories of an equivalent (by weight) helping of quiche, sausages, or pork pie, and around two thirds of the fat found in the same weight helping of pizza.

Dairy products (for example, butter and cheese) are high in fat. Items such as cream are really all fat and easy to identify, but with most foods, where the fat is found in the company of proteins or carbohydrates, it can be difficult to work out what is high-fat.

Red meat such as beef and lamb are fatty and may consequently have twice or more the calories of chicken and turkey, depending on how much fat there is on the particular cut. Game meats (pheasant, for example) are lower in fat than some red meats and therefore lower in calories, and the same applies to most fish and seafood (although seafood may, confusingly, be very high in cholesterol). Processed foods and prepared main meals may not look obviously fatty but most contain high quantities of fat – and sugar.

YOUR DAILY CALORIES

Nutrition experts suggest that the average daily calorie requirement for women aged between nineteen and fifty is around 2,000 a day, and for men (in the same age span) around 2,500 a day. However, these recommendations do vary from country to country (they are higher in the US, for example).

Beware of the number of calories you consume in the form

of fat by habitually eating what are really just accompaniments to the main dish – or nibbling between meals. A generous portion of butter or margarine on your bread or toast in the morning may add 100 calories or more to a slice of bread. With fat containing over 200 calories an ounce, you can see how very easy it is to eat too much on an everyday basis. A cream sauce to accompany fish or meat, or a helping of cream or ice cream on a pudding, sends the calorie count up by a huge amount in proportion to the main dish you are actually eating. It can easily double the amount of calories. What is giving you sustenance and filling you up is the slice of bread, the portion of meat, and the slices of fruit. But it is the constant presence of accompanying high-fat, high-calorie items that does a lot of the

> **A *generous portion* of *butter* or *margarine* on *your* bread or toast in the morning may add 100 *calories* or more to a slice of bread**

damage – much more than you might realise. It is easy to see how the average diet is composed of nearly 40 per cent fat, and how simply adjusting your food a little (leaving out the cream sauce) can make a big difference to the number of calories you eat each day.

One well-known restaurant chain, Pizza Express, now helpfully lists the calorie content of all its dishes. Before that, many customers who worried about their waistlines were used to opting for the salad niçoise instead of a pizza on the seemingly obvious assumption that this would be the better choice. But what the calorie count showed was that if you had just 28 grams (about a generous tablespoonful and a half) of the delicious creamy dressing that accompanied the salad, this brought the total calories to 818 and made it the most calorific item on the menu; the most calorific pizza offered was 780 calories.

ANALYSING YOUR FOOD DIARY

So now it's time to look at your food diary and single out all the hidden or marginal items containing a high or significant proportion of fat.

Remember that it is not just the food itself but the way it is cooked and served. Butter or soured cream on a baked potato or mayonnaise on salad are just routine ways of upping the calorie count. One problem with fat is that we have become accustomed to using it to make our food richer and more delicious. Take a hard look at the way your food is prepared. Do you regularly eat food that is fried? Or food that is served with a sauce? If you have cheese at the end of your supper, do you tend to just carry on nibbling it throughout the evening? Do you perhaps wash it down with an extra glass of wine or two? A lot of this is habit, and giving it up is not really serious deprivation. Nibble some fruit instead. Or some raw vegetables chopped up as crudités. The one thing you must beware of is having high-fat food around that you can pick at. Cheese is a particularly insidious temptation, but biscuits, crisps, and the whole range of nibbles that you can now find in the supermarket must really be banished if you want to lose weight.

Marginal calories

One way or the other, you could be consuming an alarming number of calories that really do very little to satisfy your appetite but which steadily encourage you to put on weight and will make it impossible for you to lose it. It only takes a few excess calories a day to put on lots of weight over time. If you can identify this marginal consumption and talk yourself into doing without it, you are well on the way to cutting the number of calories you eat and losing weight.

Approaching weight loss this way – seeing what you can do without – will produce much better results in the end than embarking on a suddenly strenuous new regime. With marginal consumption we are not discussing the actual *quantity* of food or the number of meals you eat, but the *choice* of foodstuffs. Eliminating these unhelpful sources of calories from your diet is really a question of mental effort rather than starvation. When you are faced with a food

> It only takes a few excess calories a day to put on lots of weight over time

choice, whether at home, in a restaurant, or in a supermarket, just pause to think before you reach for the high-fat, high-calorie item.

- Is this food item really necessary?
- How many calories does it add to your daily intake?
- Do you really like it *that* much?
- Isn't it about time you did something more original with chicken breasts than smother them with a cream sauce?
- Surely you can get through your day without crisps/cake/chocolate?
- Are you really serious about losing weight?

If you don't learn to let go of these foods you will not lose the weight you want to.

FAT AND FOOD CRAVINGS

Although reducing the amount of fat in our diet is the quickest way to reduce the calorie content of the food we eat, it is important to appreciate that small quantities of particular kinds of fat are actually good for us whilst others are best avoided. Apart from being boring, a no-fat diet can result in actual aches and pains in your joints and set off terrible food cravings leading to bingeing and general misery.

There are a number of theories why totally excluding fat from the diet stimulates food cravings. One of the most widely

> *Eat regularly; getting to the stage where you are starving hungry just decimates your will-power*

touted is that we are genetically programmed by our very early ancestors' experiences. Periods of near-starvation were punctuated by a feast of (high-fat) meat-eating when there was a kill. The human body was designed to 'stock up' in good times in preparation for the lean periods when there would be little food available. Therefore, when we eat high-fat food, our bodies automatically anticipate future starvation and lay down surplus calories as fat. (There is also a theory that women, who have a higher proportion of fat than men, store fat in order to breastfeed their young.) Another explanation, of course, is simply that a lot of high-fat food is very moreish and gratifying to eat, thanks to the food manufacturing industry and its assiduous marketing of products to catch our fancy.

Whatever the reason for food cravings, you have to come to terms with them. Once you start eating properly they will go away. It is, of course, very important to eat regularly; getting to the stage where you are starving hungry just decimates your will-power.

THE RIGHT ATTITUDE TO FAT

Some people believe that excluding all fat is bad for the skin and hair as well as for general health. We have all seen articles about olive oil being good for you – part of the Mediterranean diet that protects against heart disease.

So, just what is the correct attitude to fat? The first important distinction to make is between **saturated fats** and **unsaturated fats**, while understanding that many food items contain both kinds. It is the relative proportions that are important.

SATURATED FATS

These are found in high concentrations in animal and dairy products – butter, cheese, meat, eggs, lard, some margarines, and even some vegetable oils (coconut oil, for instance). It is fairly easy to spot saturated fat in meat from the fact that the juices (and the gravy, if you don't take steps to pour the fat off) will, as they cool to room temperature, form a skin of white fat. This saturated fat is implicated in heart disease and other circulatory disorders, so eating as little as possible is the healthy thing to do.

A doctor I know uses a graphic description to try to make his patients pay more attention to the amount of saturated fat they eat. He asks them if they have ever blocked up the kitchen sink by pouring fat down the drain and finding that it hardens. Then he asks them to imagine what it does to their arteries. It is quite an effective way of making patients visualise the impact of too much saturated fat on their system.

Saturated fats and cholesterol

Saturated fats are also believed to raise blood cholesterol levels and an excess of cholesterol could eventually clog up the vital blood vessels to and from your heart. Confusingly we need *some* cholesterol, which is actually manufactured by the body, but most of us produce more than we need to keep everything ticking along nicely. Even more confusingly, there is some debate about the role of the cholesterol found in food (as opposed to the stuff our bodies manufacture) and just what impact it has on natural cholesterol levels in the blood. Most high-cholesterol foods are also high-fat foods. Prawns and lobster are the best-known exceptions; like liver and kidneys, they are high in cholesterol but low in fat and a very useful base for a meal if you are trying to lose weight.

Foods containing a preponderance of saturated fats are not always that easy to spot. Don't run away with the idea that low-fat spreads and healthier-sounding margarines are always better for you. Margarines are just as high in calories as butter,

> **Margarines are just as high in calories as butter**

and they often contain hydrogenated vegetable oils which are best avoided since the hydrogenation process basically turns unsaturated into saturated fats. Again, processed foods frequently contain saturated or hydrogenated fats among their ingredients – primarily because the manufacturers want to use the cheapest ingredients. It's amazing what can be whipped up to make a gooey dessert.

UNSATURATED FATS

Then there are the unsaturated fats, which are split into groups and subgroups. These fats contain important nutrients called essential fatty acids which are very important to your health and well-being. Basically, these nutrients, which are now believed to have a positive therapeutic effect on a whole range of conditions from premenstrual tension to heart disease, are found in vegetable oils, oily fish, and nuts. All these items are very high in calories and you should never eat too much of them if you want to lose weight.

SUPPLEMENTS AND VITAMINS

You don't need a lot of fat to function, but you do need some and you should make sure it is the right kind. Many people, for instance, take fish oil supplements for health reasons. However, most doctors and nutritionists agree that ingesting these important nutrients (and vitamins) as part of your normal daily diet is almost certainly more effective than swallowing capsules. The supplements that are sold in the shops are not a whole food but an artificial replacement that the experts *think* does this, that, or the next thing. It is quite likely that we do not yet know everything there is to know about nutrition, and that there are other beneficial substances in food that work together with known supplements in ways we do not yet understand. This is why obtaining your nutrition from the food itself, rather than from supplements, is thought to be better.

There are several important vitamins (A, D, E, and K) in fat, too, but we can obtain them from other food instead (there is little risk of deficiency resulting from restricting consumption of fat for calorie reduction purposes).

LOWER-FAT, NOT LOW-FAT

One important thing to bear in mind is that you are trying to get yourself on to a *lower*-fat, rather than a *low*-fat, diet. You might think it's the same thing, but psychologically there is an important distinction. You have compared your food diary with the recommended structure of a balanced diet and you have probably found that you regularly have too high a proportion of fat in your diet. So the situation is not that you should go on a low-fat diet. You were eating too much high-fat food before and now you are trying to get back to something more appropriate.

The changing diet

Forget the cave-dwelling ancestors. Just three or four generations ago, our grandparents and great-grandparents simply did not have access to so much protein and processed food. Meat was relatively scarce; dairy products were relatively expensive. People ate a lot of vegetables, potatoes, and bread, and they were much thinner than we are now. Many nutritionists claim that the UK population was very healthy during the Second World War when food was rationed. This is probably a bit of an overstatement since there was a shortage of fruit most of the time, but there is an element of truth in it.

The post-war cheap food policies that created a mass market for Commonwealth meat in the UK were responsible for changing our diets and making them more unhealthy. They also made us lazy and unimaginative cooks. The French, on the other hand, did not have access to cheap meat and their health, their cuisine, and their dress sizes were all the better for it.

Much of our current food culture, concentrated as it has been on meat and dairy products, has pushed fruit, vegetables, and starchy foods into a secondary role. As we have seen, these latter items should account for two thirds of our daily diet. To reach that goal, which means that you will lose weight without even thinking about it, you must concentrate on incorporating the principle of balance into your daily food intake.

Eliminating the inessentials is just the first stage in getting back into a proper balance. Now is the time to go through your food diary again and plan how you can reduce your fat and calorie intake even more.

CHAPTER FIVE

Fat and Protein

HIGH-FAT PROTEINS

Once you have eliminated the inessentials from your diet you will have gone a long way towards reducing the amount of calories that you eat. What you should do now is try to reduce the amount of high-fat protein in your diet. Unless you are a vegetarian you will be used to regarding meat, fish, or eggs as the centre of many of your main meals and there is nothing wrong with that. These are all satisfying, delicious, and necessary things to eat. But one of the things that has caused us to change shape over the last few decades is the plentiful supply of protein, particularly high-fat proteins like meat. Many of us are over-dependent on animal protein but there is a lot we can do to cut back without feeling deprived.

- We can substitute white meat for red meat, or fish for meat.
- We can pay more attention to the actual cuts we buy.
- We can reduce the fat calories by changing the way we cook meat and fish.
- We can become more inventive in the way we incorporate meat and fish into our main meals, making smaller amounts go further.

> *Many of us are over-dependent on animal protein*

CALORIE AND FAT CONTENTS

The table below shows the comparative calorie and fat content for meat and fish. This is not designed to turn you into a furtive calorie counter; it just gives you an idea of how wide the variations in fat content can be.

A portion weighing 100g or 3.5oz is equivalent to a small skinless chicken breast (125-150g/4-5oz is the standard size on sale in most supermarkets). To put that into context, the average calorie consumption in the UK is 1,800 calories a day. Most experts reckon that for women, eating 1,000 to 1,200 calories a day is a healthy target when you are trying to lose weight. (For men the target should be 1,500 to 2,000 calories a day.)

The table helps you to identify items that you should avoid completely while you are trying to lose weight. The good news is that you can see at a glance how a simple switch – from lamb to turkey, for instance – can make a big difference to the amount of calories you consume in a day.

COMPARATIVE CALORIE AND FAT CONTENT OF MEAT AND FISH

Item	Fat grams (per 100g/3.5oz)	Calories (per 100g/3.5oz
Meat		
Bacon (grilled)	35.0	420
Beef (minced, stewed)	15.0	230
Beef (rump steak, grilled)	12.0	218
Beef (sirloin steak, roast)	21.0	284
Chicken (roast)	14.0	216
Chicken (skinless, breast, baked)	4.0	142
Duck (roast)	29.0	339
Gammon (boiled)	18.9	269

Lamb (chops, grilled)	37.1	355
Lamb (leg of, roast)	17.9	266
Liver (calves, cooked)	13.2	254
Pheasant (roast)	9.3	213
Pigeon (roast)	13.2	230
Pork (chops, lean, grilled)	10.7	226
Pork (leg, roast)	19.8	286
Pork (sausages, grilled)	24.5	318
Rabbit (stewed)	7.7	179
Turkey (roast)	6.5	170
Turkey (skinless, breast, baked)	1.4	132
Venison (roast)	6.4	198

Fish/Seafood
(baked or boiled)

Cod	1.2	96
Crab	5.2	127
Haddock	0.8	98
Halibut	4.0	131
Lobster	3.4	119
Plaice	1.9	93
Salmon	13.0	197
Smoked salmon	4.5	142
Shrimp/prawns	0.8	73
Trout	4.5	135

BUYING

Search out lean cuts of meat in the supermarket. Nowadays most stores sell premium lines of lamb, beef, and pork that have less visible fat on them. As you can see from the table above it's possible to make a huge difference to the calorie content of the meat you buy if you choose leaner cuts. You will see that items such as lamb chops are particularly high in fat.

That does not mean that you have to give up lamb; look out for steaks cut from the leg as an alternative, or lamb fillet.

Few of us have much time to shop for food, which is why it is very easy to take the line of least resistance and carry on buying the kind of items that we have always bought, simply because we know exactly what we are going to do with them when we get home. This is one of the major stumbling blocks to weight loss because it keeps you mired in the same eating routine. It takes an effort to adjust and try something different. Make up your mind what you are going to cook that night or over the next few days *before* you go shopping. Dip into your cookery books for inspiration.

TRY ORGANIC MEAT

There are a huge variety of meats now routinely available in the shops which should encourage you to substitute and experiment with different things. The main innovations on the meat counters are increasing amounts of organic meat and a wider selection of game. Because organic meat has not been fattened up artificially, it *may* be leaner than mainstream supplies – but the fat that is actually on it is just as calorific and should still be trimmed away. However, organic meat often tastes superior to the intensively farmed variety so it is worth the extra money on taste grounds alone. Nor is it stuffed full of hormones, colourings, and all the other things we are now encouraged to worry about.

SUBSTITUTING

Think about the way you can substitute foods. By trying something different you will not only make your cooking more interesting, you will also help yourself lose weight.

GAME

Many supermarkets stock a good variety of game – pheasant, rabbit, pigeon, venison, and wild duck (farmed duck is very fatty). Although a lot of game is now farmed (rather than being caught in the wild), it is a healthy, delicious choice with an air of luxury that makes it very useful as part of a diet plan.

FISH AND SHELLFISH

As you can see from the table on pages 57–8, some fish has, ounce for ounce, less than half the calories of popular meat cuts – and shellfish is very low fat indeed. Most fish is as (or more) expensive than meat, but salmon is relatively cheap and very flexible as the base for a meal. Deciding to cook two or three

> *Deciding to cook two or three fish- or seafood-based main meals each week will radically cut your calorie intake*

fish- or seafood-based main meals each week will radically cut your calorie intake and help you to lose weight.

AVOID CONVENIENCE FOODS

Do not buy processed foods and ready-prepared meals. Everything you buy should be as near its natural raw state as possible. This also means not buying any kind of self-basting joints, or meat that has been prepared as 'ready to cook', or anything that comes with stuffings, sauces, or gravies. These 'add-ons' – presumably designed to increase profit margins for the manufacturers and retailers – are where the real high-fat and high-calorie damage is likely to be inflicted on your food regime. Avoid anything in breadcrumbs, pastry, or batter.

PREPARING AND COOKING FOOD

Opinions differ about the amount of protein you need each day. Most non-vegetarians probably eat more than enough. The chicken breasts you buy in the supermarket will weigh between 125g/4oz and 150g/5oz and represent a reasonable daily intake of animal protein for most of us. You neither need, nor should you eat, more than 125–150g/4–5oz of protein in a day if you want to lose weight.

No amount of care over the kind of food you buy or the way you cook it will help you lose weight unless you are pretty strict with yourself over the amounts of protein you eat at each meal. You really have to keep an eye on it. The next time you have a piece of chicken, a chop, or a bit of steak in the kitchen ready to cook, weigh it first. Work out the approximate amount of calories and fat it contains using the table on pages 57–8. You should only have to do this exercise once, just as a guide to the future. It will help to fix in your mind the amount that it is appropriate for you to eat.

The trick is to turn modest portions of these foods into something delicious and satisfying on the plate by accessorising them with a range of vegetables and flavours.

TAKE THE FAT OFF

Even if you buy leaner cuts of meat there will probably be some fat still on them. You should always remove this before you cook them. Many people cut the fat off when the meat is actually cooked and on their plates. That is not as effective in reducing calories, because cooking meat with the fat on will make the meat itself higher in fat and you will not be able to remove all the fat so effectively since some of it will seep into the meat while cooking.

You can make a big reduction in the fat content of poultry such as chicken and turkey by taking the skin off either before or after you cook it, but doing it before is more effective. As you can see from the table above most of the fat on poultry is just under the skin. However, if you are cooking a whole bird, remove any other fat lurking in the cavity before preparing it for the oven.

It seems a sacrilege to take the fat and crackling off pork but you should. Pork has the reputation of being particularly high in fat – but it isn't if you choose the right lean cut such as loin, or take the fat off chops. Some cuts of meat, for example, breast of lamb, are best avoided altogether while you are trying to lose weight. Bacon, sadly, is an absolute no-no.

STIR-FRY DISHES

These are one good method of stretching a small amount of high-calorie protein into a substantial meal very quickly. Most supermarkets now sell a variety of packets of stir-fry vegetables that you can use as a ready-cut foundation while adding other flavours or vegetables to taste – garlic, ginger, spring onions, peppers – anything you fancy can be incorporated to jazz up the flavour. The protein – in the form of beef, pork, chicken, or prawns – turns it into a filling and satisfying meal.

Although these dishes are called stir-*fry*, only a minimal

amount of oil is used. Try sesame oil which is particularly delicious and full of flavour. Many people also use a light soy sauce. If you buy the supermarket packets of stir-fry veg, don't use the sachets they supply with them. They are not the best ingredients, they may contain a lot of sugar, and you will do better to make up your own mix.

USE YOUR GRILL

Grilling is another good method of preparing food in a way that reduces fat and makes the most of your protein base. If you want to lose weight, but enjoy cooking and eating, you must invest in a really heavy, top-quality grill pan to use on top of the stove. These have ridges that give food the attractive stripes that have become so fashionable. But the important point about these pans is that when meat is cooked in them, the fat released sinks between the ridges, away from the food. Buy a grill pan with the highest ridges, plus an oil sprayer that you can fill with your own oil to give the pan just the lightest touch to stop the food sticking – and start experimenting.

- Peppers, courgettes, and aubergines look particularly attractive sliced in long wedges and grilled along with cuts of meat or fish.
- Grill the meat or fish and vegetables together as kebabs and serve with a salad.

RING THE CHANGES

Preparing food to give different tastes and textures sounds fiddly but it can be done quite simply and quickly, particularly if you are cooking for several people and can justify having several pans on the stove at once. Here is just one idea:

Start with a base of puréed swede, just boiled to tenderness and then processed in the food processor, with a touch of walnut oil to bring out the flavour of the root vegetable. Then add a layer of stir-fried or steamed vegetables – bean sprouts, mangetout, carrots, spring onions, or French beans. Finally, add a chicken breast from the grill pan, sliced crosswise. You could marinate the chicken for flavour before you cook it (see marinades, pages 98–9), keeping some aside before adding the meat to drizzle a little over the rest of the dish. (Don't use any of the liquid in which the meat was marinated.) This makes a healthy, filling, delicious and attractive-looking dish that has taken no longer than half an hour (probably less) to prepare.

You can use many kinds of meat and fish in this way. Once you start experimenting, building your own quick, delicious meals from a wide variety of ingredients, you will not want to eat any other way. It is a very effective method of keeping in check the amount of protein you eat without feeling horribly deprived.

FLAVOUR YOUR FOOD

When retraining your eating patterns it is vital to flavour food in an interesting way. It is all too easy to get bored with eating skinned chicken breast without a delicious creamy sauce. You may be used to pouring in a carton of cream when you cook tarragon chicken, but you can get the same flavour and succulence by cooking the meat and herbs with white wine or stock instead, and you will end up with a delicious and much less calorific sauce.

No *cream sauces*
You don't have to give up your favourite dishes completely. Once you have lost the weight you want, you can substitute yoghurt or fromage frais for cream if you want a sauce. As you can see from the table on page 67, these have half the calories

of cream and you can lower the calories still more if you buy the low-fat variety.

Both **fromage frais** and **yoghurt** are delicious mixed with fresh herbs or mustards – so try your favourite recipes substituting them for cream. (A mustard or herb sauce is particularly good with grilled salmon.) But you must not get carried away with these substitute cream sauces. Ideally it's best to give up creamy sauces altogether, and treat yourself to them only occasionally.

There are plenty of ideas for sauces in Chapter Eight.

Using vegetables and fruit

Tomatoes make a wonderful base for herb and spicy sauces. But beware: tinned varieties sometimes contain sugar in the juice. Prepare your own by making a small nick in the skin and popping them in boiling water to skin them; then you can do practically anything with them.

Experiment with **fruit sauces and purées** to go with meat or fish. One of the lovely things about American cooking is the lack of inhibition when it comes to using fruit, whether in fruit and vegetable salsas or simply puréed and served as a sauce with, maybe, a dollop of wine in there somewhere.

> *Experiment with fruit sauces and purées to go with meat or fish*

My favourite recipe is for grilled wild duck breast (minus skin) with blackberry sauce. Just put some blackberries in a saucepan with a quarter of a glass of red wine and some fresh thyme and cook gently for a few minutes until the blackberries lose their shape. This is delicious on a bed of mixed lettuce in summer or over puréed spinach with crunchy mangetout or French beans in winter.

There are more recipes for vegetable and fruit sauces on pages 100–106.

> **Marinating meat or fish before cooking helps ring the flavour changes**

MARINADES

Marinating meat or fish before cooking helps ring the flavour changes. Herbs, spices, lemon juice, and different kinds of vinegars and mustards can all be used to flavour your food in delicious ways. But don't buy ready-made marinades or flavourings – they are often highly calorific, even if they are labelled low-fat, and can have a synthetic tinge to their taste. With so much in the way of fresh herbs available in the supermarket it is just as easy and quick to chop and mix your own and then you can be certain that the ingredients are the best available.

See the recipes for marinades on pages 98–100.

DAIRY PRODUCTS

Dairy products represent the other major area of high-fat protein. Milk, cheese, cream, and yoghurt are high in calories but contain essential nutrients, too. The real problem is that the way our diets have evolved means that many of us have become far too dependent on this class of food item. However, it is wrong to condemn a whole range of foods; as with the other food groups, it is a question of restoring a good balance.

Women are constantly told that they should eat dairy products because these foods contain **calcium**, which guards against osteoporosis (the brittle-bone disease that may afflict women during and after the menopause). In fact, calcium is found in a wide range of non-dairy food including fruit, vegetables, and nuts. In order to protect the body and its bones, the calcium has to interact with other minerals such as magnesium. Shortage of some of these other trace elements is probably as much of an issue as a lack of calcium for most of the female population. As ever the answer lies in enjoying as healthy a diet as possible – eating a wide range of fresh, unadulterated foods – and not just worrying about calcium intake.

The table below shows the calorie and fat content of a range of dairy food. It is not designed to turn you into a frantic calorie counter but is just a reminder of how easy it is to put on weight by eating seemingly small amounts of these items. You really can add hundreds of calories to your normal daily diet almost without noticing.

COMPARATIVE CALORIE AND FAT CONTENT OF DAIRY PRODUCTS

Item	Fat (per 100g/3.5oz)	Calories (per 100g/3.5oz)
Double cream	48.0	449
Yoghurt	3.0	79
Yoghurt (Greek)	9.1	115
Yoghurt (low-fat)	0.8	56
Fromage frais (low-fat)	50.0	110
Butter	80.0	720
Cheeses		
Brie	27.0	319
Cheddar	34.4	412
Camembert	23.7	297
Edam	25.4	333
Stilton	35.5	411

MAKING HEALTHY CHOICES

Milk

If you want to lose weight you should switch to skimmed milk, and stay switched. It contains all the nutrients and calcium of full-fat milk, but is minus most of the fat and works out at half the calories.

> *Switch to skimmed milk, and stay switched*

Cheese

Keep cheese-eating to the absolute minimum. If you are a real cheese fan, that can be tough. Frankly, for those who like their Stilton and Brie, there is no low-fat substitute that could possibly be worth eating, and a good cheese is one of those things that it is very difficult to just eat a little of at a time. Unless you have an iron will, forget about eating cheese; banish it from the kitchen while you are concentrating on losing weight. When you are on a maintenance diet, treat cheese like a protein, the centre of your protein-based meal for the day, and eat it with salad or fruit. Don't eat it in addition to a main meal.

> *Keep cheese-eating to the absolute minimum*

Butter and cream

These should both be banned, too. A glance at the table will tell you that they are both just pure fat. And be warned: many butter substitutes are as calorific as butter, as are allegedly healthy, polyunsaturated spreads. Do you really need any of them at all? Isn't it habit that makes you spread butter or margarine on your bread?

However, plain **yoghurt** makes a good substitute for cream. This is, in fact, one of the few substitutions worth trying because yoghurt is so delicious anyway and you may end up preferring it. Spending time reading labels and counting calories is depressing. It really is easier not to eat the obviously high-fat and high-calorie items highlighted by the tables. Don't make it hard for yourself by tempting your hard-won will-power.

Nuts
Nuts contain important nutrients, but they are very high in fat, very moreish, and best left alone while you are trying to lose weight.

VEGETARIANS

If you are vegetarian, nuts and cheese are good providers of protein, as are avocados, which are also high in fat. So vegetarians should eat these – although in the same restricted amounts that non-vegetarians eat meat. Non-vegetarians should try to cut down further on these foods while trying to lose weight.

ACCENTUATE THE POSITIVE

Concentrate on what you *can* eat and experiment with new flavours and ways of cooking. As I've mentioned, one reason why it can be so hard to lose weight is that we get into a rut with food. Our weight-loss diets can become very boring unless we take on new ideas and ways of doing things. Make a promise to yourself to try one or two new dishes a week. Once you develop new habits to replace the old ones, you will find that you do not want to go back to your old way of eating.

Turn the process of losing weight into a more interesting

It is important that you find food that you can enjoy eating, otherwise you will not manage to lose weight and positive experience. It is important that you find food that you can enjoy eating, otherwise you will not manage to lose weight. Once you find the right balance, you'll have a much better chance of keeping off surplus weight in the future.

CHAPTER SIX

Carbohydrates: Friend or Foe?

THE SLIMMER'S ENEMY

Once upon a time carbohydrates were regarded as the slimmer's major enemy. When you wanted to lose weight the accepted wisdom was that you had to cut back on starches, like bread, pasta, and potatoes, as well as sugary foods. Then it all changed. Sugar was still out but bread, pasta, and rice became the Holy Trinity of the diet culture – the source of all good things. In between times there have been variations on the theme, notably the idea that dieters should increase their intake of high-fibre foods. This sparked off an orgy of baked potato eating and bran sprinkling throughout the Western world.

Then, again, there are plenty of counter-theories: for example, the carbohydrate evangelists have it all wrong and you should begin a high-protein diet or even a high-fat diet regime. Another popular theme is that carbohydrates should not be mixed with protein, the basis of food-combining.

FOOD-COMBINING

Food-combining diets rule that proteins – particularly animal proteins – and starchy foods should not be eaten together, and produce some complicated chemistry to show that these two different foods 'fight' each other as they are digested.

Diets based on these kind of food-combining theories can get immensely complicated. They are the antithesis of *No Fuss Fat Loss* and are certain to fail unless you become completely hooked on the system they propound and are prepared to be very dedicated. Not necessarily a healthy state of mind; and these systems can be nutritionally restrictive.

CONFUSED?

Carbohydrates are the biggest food group and contain the good, the bad, and the ugly. They include starchy foods (for example, bread, rice, and pasta), sugary items such as jams and honey, as well as fruit, vegetables, beans, and cereals. A carbohydrate food is defined as one that contains more carbohydrate than anything else – some contain substantial amounts of vegetable protein, fibre, and vitamins as well. Only a few carbohydrates have measurable amounts of fat. Carbohydrates are the body's main source of energy. All the food you eat, including protein and fat, is broken down into carbohydrate compounds before being absorbed. Carbohydrate foods, which are broken down into glucose, are the easiest food for the body to assimilate and use quickly. According to the high-carbohydrate, low-fat lobby, it is the fuel and food group of choice.

Sugar is the ultimate empty calorie – the energy source without anything else to recommend it

So are all carbohydrate foods good for you? Well, obviously not. There are carbohydrates and carbohydrates. In fact, when you look at the range of carbohydrate foods they are very varied indeed.

Sugar – the white granulated stuff we put in our coffee and tea and which is loaded into fizzy drinks and sweets – is carbohydrate and provides energy. But despite the most lavishly financed efforts of the sugar manufacturing industry, no one has yet come up with a sound nutritional reason why we ever need to eat it at all. Sugar is the ultimate empty calorie – the energy source without anything else to recommend it: no vitamins, no fibre, no handy trace elements lurking there to justify its existence in our diet. Yet it is everywhere. Not only is it obviously present in cakes, biscuits, and a whole range of high-fat foods, it is also used in a lot of manufactured, processed, or tinned savoury food to make the flavour more tempting. This is the major reason why you should avoid all commercially prepared food, not just cakes and chocolate, if you want to lose weight.

CARBOHYDRATES: THE FACTS

Whole books have been written on the wonders of carbohydrates. But there are one or two basic facts that dieters need to become acquainted with.

BLOOD SUGAR LEVELS

Sugar is what is known as a simple carbohydrate – broken down by the body very quickly. It provides instant energy. That is why people are sometimes given glucose (the molecular form in which the body actually absorbs sugar) when they are exhausted. When people are in this state their blood sugar levels can be very low. Glucose raises the level of blood sugar quickly, so they start to feel energised again. This, of course, is in a crisis situation, but the process is not so very different from what happens inside your body when it is given a substantial amount of sugary food. Yes, you feel 'up' and ener-

Eat the right food regularly so that your blood sugar level is as stable as possible. That way, you will manage to avoid nibbling, snacking, and bingeing

gised – for a while. Insulin is then released into the body to bring down the soaring blood sugar level with a bump, setting up the need for another sugar fix. This is one reason why people become semi-addicted to chocolate and sweets and the high it gives them. It also explains why many people become faint and dizzy when they go without food, or develop cravings and start to feel desperately hungry. Their blood sugar level is low. In this state you will be prepared to eat anything and everything, so don't let it happen while you're dieting! Eating regularly, but well, actually helps weight loss.

To lose weight successfully you need to make sure that you eat the right food regularly so that your blood sugar level is as stable as possible and does not go up and down wildly. That way, you will manage to avoid nibbling, snacking, and bingeing.

FRUIT AND FIBRE

Confusingly, the fresh fruit we are advised to eat contains the kind of sugars that make them simple carbohydrates, too. So why doesn't eating fruit have the same bad effects on us as eating sugar? Fruit contains a high proportion of fibre and the body consequently takes longer to digest it. That is why many health experts disapprove of fruit juices – even 100 per cent pure unsweetened varieties – as an alternative to eating fruit. Sure, they contain the vitamin C we expect in our fruit but juice drinkers miss out on some of the other major benefits of fresh fruit eating such as fibre.

COMPLEX CARBOHYDRATES

This highlights one of the most important things about carbohydrates when considering their role in health and diet. In terms of energy, calorie for calorie, all carbohydrates are indeed equal. But whilst sugar is nutritionally useless and doesn't satisfy your hunger pangs, other carbohydrates are hugely helpful and nutritionally necessary if you want to lose weight.

The importance of carbohydrates in weight loss, however, has usually focused on the benefits of eating bread, pasta, cereals, and potatoes. These complex carbohydrates have been presented as the basis of a good diet, the dieter's friend.

The American Food Guide Pyramid, produced by the US Department of Health, shows this conventional wisdom most graphically. Here these foods are depicted as the base of what is the official 'good diet' guide.

THE FOOD GUIDE PYRAMID

Fats, oils and sweets
USE SPARINGLY

Milk, yoghurt and
cheese group
2-3 SERVINGS

Meat, poultry, fish,
dry beans, eggs
and nuts group
2-3 SERVINGS

Vegetable group
3-5 SERVINGS

Fruit group
2-4 SERVINGS

Bread, cereal, rice and pasta group
6-11 SERVINGS

The UK equivalent, the British Food Guide Plate produced by the Department of Health, shows a roughly similar pattern. The same category of food takes up an optimum one third of the desirable daily intake.

THE FOOD GUIDE PLATE

FRUIT AND VEGETABLES
choose a wide variety

BREAD, OTHER CEREALS AND POTATOES
eat all types and choose high fibre kinds whenever you can

PASTA

MEAT, FISH AND ALTERNATIVES
choose lower fat alternatives whenever you can

FATTY AND SUGARY FOODS
try not to eat these too often, and when you do, have small amounts

TOFFEE

MILK AND DAIRY FOODS
choose lower fat alternatives whenever you can

But just as fruit, composed of simple sugars, actually turns out to be a very good thing to eat despite its sugar chemistry, some of the foods that fall into the officially desirable complex-carbohydrate category should be treated with caution. Don't fall for the notion that it is OK to eat huge amounts of them, despite all the hype. It might be all right for physically hard-working peasants to eat lots of pasta, rice, and potatoes. Contemporary sedentary urbanites live a completely different and far less active life. We simply do not need all that carbohydrate – unless we work on a farm or want to run the marathon.

High-carbohydrate diets are the food of choice for international footballers and other sports stars who need masses of energy to train or play every day, but most of us don't fall into this category. These food items, which we are all encouraged to think of as the basics of a healthy diet, are basically high-calorie fillers, modestly laced with nutritional goodies. Whatever the diet gurus say, common sense suggests that eating unrestricted amounts of bread, pasta, and rice is not the way to lose weight. One way or the other, excess calories, from whatever source, end up stored in our bodies as fat.

This is why hundreds of thousands of dieters who have tried these kinds of high-carbohydrate diets have failed to lose weight. In fact, many people who have dutifully struggled with high-carbohydrate diets have found that by simply giving up eating bread, for instance, they have managed the kind of speedy, gratifying loss of a few pounds that previously eluded them. It is not hard to see why.

Wheat allergy is a popular diagnosis when people seek help in order to lose weight. Most bread, pasta, and breakfast cereal is wheat-based, and wheat, like fat and sugar, is one of the great staples of the food manufacturing industry. Persuade someone that they need to cut out wheat and you immediately remove a huge long list of foods from the menu, which inevitably results in an instant reduction in calories. The truth, of course, is that it is daft to ban a whole group of foods like this, except in the (rare) case of genuine allergy. It comes back to a question of balance.

Many people do report that **bread** makes them feel bloated. There is, in fact, plenty of anecdotal evidence to suggest that foods such as bread, which have been hailed as wonder nosh in diet circles for years, should be eaten with restriction and caution, and should not be regarded as the central part of any healthy diet.

The same applies to **white rice, baked potatoes,** and **pasta**. It does not mean that we cannot eat them if we are on a diet. It is just that their reputation as some kind of magic fat-burning fodder has been completely exaggerated.

THE GLYCAEMIC INDEX

Scientists have come up with Glycaemic Index tables listing carbohydrate foods to show which ones are absorbed into the body gradually and which ones raise blood sugar levels more quickly. The quicker the carbohydrate food raises the blood glucose level, the higher it ranks on the Glycaemic Index. Along with neat sugar and chocolate bars, potatoes, white bread, pasta, and rice are up there near the top of the list. Eaten in the kind of quantities that are frequently recommended by weight loss experts, these foods spell death to any long-term effort to diet because they play havoc with the body's blood sugar levels and can stimulate us to eat more food – and the wrong kind of food at that. As we have seen, soaring blood sugar levels result in the release of insulin to bring them down. However, not only does over-dependence on these starchy foods result in the blood sugar ups and downs that make us feel hungry, frazzled, and subject to food cravings, but many nutritionists also believe that this pattern actually encourages the body to store fat since lower blood sugar levels are a hunger signal. Essentially it all goes back to our feast and famine programming.

HOW MUCH?

Really, if you want to lose weight you should have no more than *one helping* of just *one* of these starchy carbohydrates each day. In the current dieting culture this is heresy, but readers who have tried and failed to lose weight on high-carbohydrate diets will know it is common sense.

If you must eat bread, have a slice or two from a wholemeal loaf for breakfast or lunch but do not have any more helpings of starchy carbohydrates that day. But don't despair: there are plenty of carbohydrate foods that you can eat in abundance.

REFINED CARBOHYDRATES

What carbohydrates can offer us, apart from energy, is:

- **Bulk** – to stop us feeling hungry
- **Fibre** – to fill us up and keep our digestive system in shape
- **Nutrients** – such as vitamins, minerals, calcium, and iron

Bread, potatoes, pasta, and rice are not the only effective way of obtaining the above and are very far from being the best sources. Bread, pasta and rice are usually highly refined, which drastically reduces the nutrients and the fibre you get from them. Many nutrients are stripped away by the process of food production. This is one reason why these foods figure high up on the Glycaemic Index, identifying them as food items that raise the blood sugar quickly, rather than help to maintain the steady blood sugar level we need to help us control our eating and appetite. These foods are absorbed more quickly because they have lost so much of their original fibre during the production process. They may have the same amount of calories as their unrefined equivalent but their impact on what might be called our 'eating ecology' is much less beneficial.

> *Bread, pasta and rice are usually highly refined, which drastically reduces the nutrients and the fibre you get from them*

The Glycaemic Index really demonstrates why it is a mistake to pay too much attention to the notion that healthy peasants stayed thin and fit on a high carbohydrate diet. Most of the carbohydrate food they ate was quite different from the food we eat now. It was unrefined and unprocessed, which makes all the difference to its dietary role.

Whilst wholemeal bread is widely available and delicious, unrefined pasta and rice is neither easy nor quick to cook, and many people do not find it particularly appealing to eat. Essentially these are all fairly bland-tasting foods that we must eat with something else to make them interesting, and that 'something else' is usually highly calorific.

UNREFINED CARBOHYDRATES

There are other carbohydrate foods that can provide much the same benefits as pasta, rice, bread, and potatoes but with more nutritional value and much more taste: fruit and vegetables. Far from being bland, they offer a huge range of gorgeous flavours and most of them are packed full of vitamins and fibre. They are mostly low calorie and have no fat – the well-known exception being avocadoes, which are high in protein and fat. It is these unrefined carbohydrates – and the different beans and pulses on offer – rather than bread, pasta, rice, and potatoes, that should be the cornerstone of our diet if we want to lose weight.

> **Reducing** the amount of fat we eat is the first rule of losing weight.
> **Increasing** the amount of fruit and vegetables we eat is the second.

THE HEALTH BENEFITS

As we can see from the American food pyramid and its British equivalent, official health advice on both sides of the Atlantic is that a good diet should contain a *minimum* of five servings of fruit and vegetables a day, and many medical experts reckon that up to ten helpings a day is really what we need for optimum health, since fruit and vegetables contain such high quantities of nutrients.

It is hard to exaggerate the nutritional and health value of these other carbohydrates – beans, pulses, fruit, and vegetables. Red kidney beans and lentils contain high quantities of protein as well as fibre which make them particularly useful foods for vegetarians, who are frequently over-dependent on much higher-fat items such as cheese for protein. Food items like beans can be easily incorporated into a salad or a casserole to provide bulk.

Militant meat eaters are frequently scathing about beans and pulses because these items have become so closely associated with vegetarian food and attitudes – the 'nut cutlet culture' that unrepentant carnivores find rather tedious. Think of these items in a different way – as much tastier substitutes for pasta, rice, and potatoes – and you will find the idea more palatable.

Fresh fruit and vegetables contain not only vitamins but also nutrients like calcium, iron, potassium, and magnesium. All these nutrients are needed to keep bones, blood, and the rest of the body healthy, renewed, and functioning properly. Because the dairy lobby has been so vocal, most people do not realise, for instance, that many green vegetables are good sources of calcium and iron.

People who are trying to lose weight frequently worry that by cutting down on food or changing their diet they will not get enough vitamins and minerals and will need to take supplements. Actually, the reverse is the case. By eating more fresh fruit and vegetables and a wider variety of food generally, you give yourself a much better chance of getting regular quantities of the nutrients you need.

ARE YOU EATING ENOUGH?

Look at your food diary again. Are you matching that minimum of five helpings of fruit and vegetables each day? Are you anywhere near the amount of ten helpings?

So far you have concentrated on cutting down, substituting and switching. Now you have to make an effort to increase the amount of fruit and vegetables you eat on a daily basis. The easiest way to do this is to incorporate fresh fruit or vegetables (or both) into absolutely every meal you eat.

We have become used to the idea that we must fall back on bread, pasta, rice, or potatoes to give bulk to a meal, but fruit and vegetables (and beans and pulses) are actually very filling. You often hear people complaining that they are hungry just a couple of hours after having a rice-based meal. That is no surprise since standard white rice is towards the high end of the Glycaemic Index. As we have seen, this means that it enters the bloodstream very rapidly, sending blood sugar levels up to begin with, then down again just as fast as insulin is released to lower the blood sugar levels. The body responds by telling you it is hungry. This does not mean that you should not eat white rice (or pasta or potatoes which have the same effect); it simply means that you should eat them at just one meal a day, not base your whole daily diet around them as many slimmers have been encouraged to do.

> *Are you matching that minimum of five helpings of fruit and vegetables each day?*

Fruit and vegetables, on the other hand, are 'slow-burn' foods with, in the main, low glycaemic ratings. This means that you should make sure you eat some of them at every meal in order to keep your blood sugar levels stable. They have, in addition, relatively high quantities of fibre and often take longer to eat.

In addition, fruit and vegetables can be much easier to prepare, since fruit is usually eaten raw and many vegetables are more nutritious in their raw state, or just lightly cooked.

You are not going to go hungry by making fruit and vegetables the cornerstone of your No Fuss Fat Loss diet. You can eat as much of them as you like since they contain no fat. Once you make that important change, incorporating as many fruits and vegetables into your daily diet as you can, you will have established an easy and satisfying way of eating that will ensure that you lose weight and keep it off.

CHAPTER SEVEN

Getting and Keeping the Balance

A DAILY DIET STRUCTURE

The key to losing weight is to give yourself an easy-to-live-with daily diet structure. Of course, this means that there will be a certain amount of predictability while you are losing weight – particularly after a few weeks. But diets that promise you excitements on a par with a culinary *Kama Sutra* are basically dishonest. If you want that, you should take a cookery course in Tuscany; it has nothing to do with the business of losing weight.

What you need is not masses of new-fangled recipes but an easily organised structure which ensures that you eat the right things every day. You will be adjusting the contents of your fridge, taking on board a higher proportion of fruit and vegetables, and buying new varieties to help make food more interesting. Just don't get trapped into thinking that you have to eat meals involving lots of complicated preparation.

Three meals a day
It is very important that you eat a proper meal three times a day. Apart from fruit and vegetables, your daily diet should have some concentrated protein (meat, fish, or eggs), chosen with an eye to its fat content, and no more than one, or at the most two, helpings of either bread, potatoes, pasta, or rice.

KEEP IT SIMPLE

Many diet books produce daily menus with different items or patterns of eating – fruit one day for breakfast, oatmeal another. This is really a way to juggle the various diet ingredients in order to make them look more varied and exciting. But busy people who have better things to do than worry about what they should and should not eat can simplify things very easily: focus on **one** of the three food groups – fruit and vegetables, carbohydrates, and proteins – at each meal.

At the most basic level, this is the foundation of the food-combining regimes mentioned earlier, although they are much more complicated than that. They do usually ensure that you eat fewer calories, but most of us will not want to spend time on this kind of pseudo-scientific homework. It is, however, worth thinking about different food combinations and the impact on your feeling of well-being that different foods have when eaten at different times of the day.

Many people find a bread and meat combination (as in a chicken sandwich or a hamburger) a little indigestible – particularly if they eat that kind of combination in the evening. You may notice this effect more as you get older. In any case, there is one very simple reason not to eat proteins and starches at the same meal. Both are filling and satisfying, so it makes sense to eat them at different meals each day. That way, you easily establish a balanced approach to your daily eating.

As you adopt the kind of simple structure suggested in this book you will become more conscious of the effect of food, and different kinds of food, on the way you feel. This is because you are likely to be eating foods from no more than two food groups at any one time. Many people find they are much more comfortable with this way of eating – and it certainly makes dieting much easier if you know what food groups you should be choosing from for each meal.

One of the most important elements in the *No Fuss* diet is increasing the amount of fruit and vegetables you eat. The simplest way to do this is to start the day with a **fruit breakfast.**

BREAKFAST

This is one of the most habit-forming meals of the day in the sense that whilst we are keen to try something new at lunch or dinner, we want breakfast to be a reassuring event. There we are, bleary eyed and in a rush to drive to work or catch the bus or train. We cling on to our coffee, toast, and marmalade, or comforting cereal – it is part of our support system.

A fruit breakfast is possibly the easiest meal of all to organise. There is no fat in fruit so basically you can eat as much as you want and the calorie count will still be very low in comparison with virtually any other food you can think of. Having a fruit breakfast also ensures that you will probably eat two or three of the desirable five to ten helpings of fruit and vegetables a day.

You needn't have the fruit just on its own. A dollop of plain (as opposed to fruit or flavoured) low-fat yoghurt is absolutely delicious with fruit and the creamy texture is quite comforting early in the morning.

One really good thing about fruit is that it does not automatically lead to our loading up with other unhelpful items. Toast, even the best and most politically correct wholemeal variety, does beg for butter and marmalade or honey, doesn't it? While you are losing weight you should not keep reminding yourself of these delights by having toast with a miserable film of low-fat chemical on it. What on earth is the point?

BREAKFAST MYTHS

No doubt you have heard that you should eat a good, filling breakfast – that the calories we take in first thing in the morning are 'worked off' during the day. There may be a certain amount of truth in that but it is not an invitation to stuff yourself with a whole lot of high-fat or high-calorie food. If you are eating these kinds of foods at breakfast, this must change if you want to lose weight. Many favourite cereals are loaded with sugar – and you should not immediately assume that any product labelled 'muesli' is worth eating, either.

> *Many people find that a starchy and/or sugary breakfast leaves them feeling very hungry by mid-morning*

It is a bit of a myth, too, to think that toast and marmalade, or even porridge, is more filling or substantial than a fresh fruit salad for breakfast. Many people find that a starchy and/or sugary breakfast leaves them feeling very hungry by mid-morning – and no wonder. As we have seen, the kind of carbohydrates found in bread and cereals are not necessarily the slow-burn, sustaining foods that we have been encouraged to believe they are. Many fruits, by contrast, have just those virtues.

Psychological factors have a lot to do with how we feel about food – and we have all been conditioned as to what is appropriate to eat. All I will say is that you should try switching to a fruit breakfast while you are losing weight. You will find that fruit such as apples and melons are easy to eat, very filling, and much more comforting to start your day with than, for example, grapefruits, which are traditionally associated with breakfast meals.

Fruit, and indeed vegetables, have long been accepted as breakfast foods for the peoples of the southern and eastern Mediterranean whose eating habits, we are constantly told, are an example to us all. It is a myth that people here have evolved a light breakfast because of the heat. As travellers know, continental buffet breakfast tables groan not just with fruit and vegetables but with cheese and eggs and olives – but bread and starchy foods are not much in evidence at all. Again it is advertising from the food processing industry (not to mention all that industrialised farming of grain) that has convinced the rest of us that cereals are the right food to eat in the morning – and it is hogwash.

Which fruit?

Some diet gurus get very fussy about which fruit should be eaten by itself, or even what kinds of fruit can – and cannot – be eaten at all. Essentially you should choose the fruit you enjoy eating. Some people, it is true, find that citrus fruit seems to unsettle them. Others do not like melons, for instance, although you should try them because whilst they are very low in calories, their high water content makes them very filling.

> *Aim for the widest variety of fruit you enjoy*

Basically, you should aim for the widest variety of fruit you enjoy – have two or three different fruits each day for breakfast. You will soon find out which fruit your system finds most satisfying. And there is so much to choose from in the supermarkets now – we can get everything virtually all the year round.

Begin with weekends

The idea of a fruit-based breakfast is very simple, but because we are so emotionally attached to what we eat for breakfast, you might find this seemingly easy step the most difficult thing to cope with in the whole *No Fuss* diet. If it does seem to be a problem, start by trying it out at weekends when you are more relaxed. A weekend is a very good time to start a diet since you can separate what is *important* (losing weight long term) from what is *urgent*

> *A weekend is a very good time to start a diet*

(all the things you have to do at work). Again, it must be stressed that this is not the Big Bang approach to dieting with which you may be familiar. There is a lot to be said for making adjustments more slowly, one at a time. As going over to a fruit-based breakfast may be the biggest single change you have to make, you might want to leave the reorganisation of this meal until last.

YOUR PROTEIN MEAL

Your protein meal, whenever you have it, should be eaten with vegetables, salads, fruits – not with other carbohydrates such as starches, which will be needed to form the basis of one of your other main meals of the day. This framework gives you a lot to choose from and just that one simple rule ensures that you can have healthy, filling meals every day at lunch and at supper which include all the important food groups in a good balance. You will not end up eating too much starchy food or too much protein. Your diet will be properly balanced – and you will hardly have to think about it.

You will probably find that you change the time at which you have your protein-based meal from day to day. On Monday it might be at a business lunch. The next day you might cook it for yourself and your family in the evening. It helps to decide the night before or at the start of each day whether lunch or supper is going to be your protein-based meal and plan your diet for the day around that.

YOUR OTHER MAIN MEAL

For your other main meal each day, you can have bread, pasta, rice, or potatoes and as many vegetables and as much fruit as you want. If, for instance, you plan to have a protein-based meal in the evening, have a salad sandwich and fruit for lunch.

Here are a few pointers:

- **Don't** prepare pasta with a meat, cream, or cheese sauce. This really loads on the calories.
- **Don't** use semi-prepared items such as savoury rice as a base. They often contain calorific items like sugar.
- **Don't** have more than one or two starchy items a day. One good helping with vegetables should be satisfying.
- **Do** try to vary your diet using different starches each day.

You may find that you prefer to have your protein meal at lunch and your starchy meal in the evening. Some people feel sleepy after a pasta meal and whilst it is OK to feel like that in the evening, you need to be alert during the day at work. Find out what suits you best. There is no particular right or wrong way round. As long as you stick to the overall structure, your diet will work for you.

EATING OUT

- If you are eating in a restaurant with others, it's perfectly allowable to choose two starters instead of a starter and a main course.
- Whatever you do, ignore the bread basket – go for vegetable crudités instead by all means but ignore the olives unless you can restrict yourself to just one or two.
- Beware of main courses that come with a sauce.
- If everyone else is having pudding, just ask for fresh fruit.

COOKING AT HOME

It will help if you can shop for food every day, or every couple of days. Not only will the food be fresher, you will also be freer to buy just what you fancy (within the rules) that day. It is a mistake just to rely on doing one big shop a week. Unless you are super-organised, you will inevitably find that your shopping expedition has set the agenda for your diet for the week, which is really not the best way round.

You will also want to vary your protein and veg routine by trying different varieties of each to make things more interesting. There is no need for you to ditch your recipe books – indeed, you can buy more of them and choose dishes that you can adapt to suit your diet. This way, you will gradually discover how to cook with ingredients that may be less familiar – and recipe books are a great source of ideas.

Gradually, you should adjust your proteins so that you eat more fish and seafood (bought fresh each day) and less meat. Meals using eggs (for example, omelettes) count as a protein dish and should just be accompanied by vegetables or salad (or both).

Cooking for the family

Life will be easy enough if you only have yourself to feed. But you have to think for more than one if you have a family. Be selfish and base the family evening meal around food that it suits you to eat. If the family complain too loudly, you will have to steel yourself not to eat starches such as rice or potatoes if you are having a protein and vegetable-based meal.

Snacks

Of course, sometimes you will get hungry between meals. This may be psychological. You are going to have to make some changes to your diet (otherwise you are going to continue to put on weight) and this may well make you feel deprived, even if you are eating filling food at the right times. If you have been used to grazing, rather than having structured meals, or if you usually grab biscuits and chocolate bars when you feel a pang

Keep crudités, or fruit such as grapes, strawberries or cherries to hand – things that you can pick at while you prepare food

of hunger, actually having an appetite before a meal may be a new experience. Most diet books rave on about how you will never be hungry on this or that regime. Well, you have to be hungry *sometime* – that is what makes eating food so thoroughly enjoyable, after all. There is a difference between anticipation and the awful hunger that comes when you force yourself on to a starvation diet.

In between meals you can eat fruit or raw vegetables. Keep crudités, or fruit such as grapes, strawberries or cherries to hand – things that you can pick at while you prepare food in the kitchen. Just stay off calorific titbits! If you really feel you need something else in between meals, have one crispbread in the morning and one in the afternoon; so long as you don't spread anything on it, you won't damage your diet.

CHAPTER EIGHT

Salsas, Sauces and Salad Dressings

SUBSTITUTE RECIPES

Many diet books have pages of recipes, many of them rather ghastly attempts to mimic highly calorific dishes. I once saw a recipe for Southern Fried Chicken that would have taken all day to prepare and cook, by the time you'd fiddled around with all the low-calorie substitutes, and it would still have ended up as a mockery of what it ought to be.

> *Don't torture yourself with pretend versions of high-calorie favourites*

While you are trying to lose weight, don't torture yourself with pretend versions of high-calorie favourites. Look, instead, for ways to liven up basic fish, chicken, pasta, and vegetable dishes by using sauces, dips, and salad dressings. There are plenty to be found that don't need butter, cream, or oil. The suggestions below have been chosen because they are easy and quick to make. They are what they are, not a low-calorie version of something else. Most of the recipes are based on vegetables, herbs, or fruit and have a wonderful flavour.

Unless otherwise stated, the recipes serve two.

SALSAS

These are absolutely brilliant when you are aiming for a healthy, low-fat, low-calorie diet and you want a really tasty alternative to buttery or creamy sauces. Salsas are crunchier than a sauce – they are more like a relish that started life as a salad and are wonderful with either hot or cold food. Tomatoes are the staple ingredient of a salsa, plus chillies and whatever else you want to throw in, including fruit. They are simple and quick to make and require no cooking at all. Salsas are particularly good with fish and chicken, and there are lots of different variations. All you have to remember is to avoid the salsa recipes that call for high amounts of olive oil.

Beware Salsa Verde – a classic mix of parsley, anchovies, garlic, capers, lemon juice, and basil. It is heavy on the olive oil and despite its name is really a sauce in the high-fat, continental tradition – lovely, but you should give it a very wide berth while dieting. You may see other salsas with avocado in the ingredients. Avocadoes, while packed full of protein, are very high in fat and are best avoided while you are losing weight.

Here are a few ideas for salsas.

Simplest Salsa
6 really ripe tomatoes
half a red onion or 1 bunch of spring onions
1 or 2 small fresh red or green chillies, depending on your taste
a good helping of fresh coriander
juice of 1 lime
salt and pepper

If you want to skin your tomatoes, make a small slit in them and put them in boiling water for a minute; afterwards the skins should come off easily. You can remove the seeds if you prefer. Some people like to use the whole tomato, just removing the paler, tougher part inside that attaches the tomato to the stem.

Finely chop the tomatoes. Finely chop the onion, chilli, and coriander, and mix them all together with the tomatoes and the lime juice. Add salt and black pepper to taste as you are mixing.

Spanish Salsa
6 really ripe tomatoes
half a red onion
1 green pepper
half a cucumber
1 clove of garlic
Tabasco

Skin and de-pip the tomatoes. Finely chop all the ingredients as before. Mix and season with salt, pepper, and a splash of Tabasco.

Mango Salsa
6 really ripe tomatoes
1 medium mango
1 bunch of spring onions
half a cucumber
juice of 1 lime

Skin and de-pip the tomatoes as before. Finely chop all the ingredients and mix together. Season with salt and pepper.

MARINADES

Marinating fish or meat for a couple of hours before cooking gives them a lovely flavour. The trouble is that many recipes for marinades require olive oil and are off limits when you are trying to lose weight. But there are alternatives.

Lemon Marinade (for chicken breasts)
1 clove of garlic, crushed
juice of 1 lemon
1 glass of white wine
1 teaspoon oregano (or fresh parsley), chopped

Mix all the ingredients together and pour over skinned chicken breasts. Leave to marinate for 2-3 hours before cooking.

Tomato Marinade (for fish)
1 cup of tomato juice
1 onion
½ teaspoon Worcestershire sauce
a few basil leaves
salt and pepper

Liquidise all the ingredients in a food processor and pour over fish. Leave to marinate for 2 hours before baking.

Five-Spice Marinade (for pork)
1 teaspoon five-spice powder
1 clove of garlic, crushed
1 teaspoon salt
1 teaspoon honey
2 tablespoons orange juice

Mix the five-spice powder with the garlic and salt and rub it on the meat. Melt the honey in a saucepan with the orange juice and pour over the meat. Leave to marinate for at least 1 hour before cooking.

SAUCES

Sauces can make a dish. A sauce makes a meal moist, succulent, and inviting, and it can transform the taste and the appearance of a simple dish of vegetables or pasta. If you are grilling meat and fish, as suggested earlier, you will find that having a variety of sauces you can whizz up in a few minutes makes all the difference.

VEGETABLE SAUCES

Red Pepper Sauce
This is lovely with chicken and vegetables. With its good warm colour it also looks rather spectacular on the plate. There are a number of versions of red pepper sauce, some of them listing crème fraiche among the ingredients. But you can make a no-fat sauce that is just as good using water, vegetable stock, or tomatoes as the liquid element to get the right consistency.

1 red pepper
1 onion
2 ripe tomatoes
1 clove of garlic, crushed
salt and pepper
1 cup of vegetable stock or water
a handful of fresh chopped herbs
Tabasco (optional)

Cut the pepper into quarters, removing the seeds. Put the pepper quarters under a very hot grill so that the skin is blackened. Then let them cool down for a few minutes until you can slip the skins off and chop them into smaller pieces.

Finely chop the onion and cook gently until transparent in a pan with a little olive oil – just enough to stop it sticking and burning (a spray is useful for this). Put the tomatoes in boiling water to remove the skins and deseed. Add the tomato flesh to the pan with the peppers plus the garlic, salt and pepper, and stock. Bring to the boil, then cook gently for about 20 minutes.

Liquidise the whole lot in the food processor, adding more liquid if needed and the herbs, plus a splash of Tabasco if you like it.

Variation

You can make **Yellow Pepper Sauce** in exactly the same way – it is just as delicious.

Tomato Sauce

A good tomato sauce is a great standby. You can use it with fish, white meat, vegetables, or pasta. It can be a simple blend of tomato, onion, and stock, or it can include other vegetables and herbs such as basil, as in this recipe.

6 ripe tomatoes
1 small onion
1 clove of garlic
1 carrot (optional)
1 celery stick (optional)
2 tablespoons tomato purée
150ml/5fl oz vegetable stock or water
fresh basil, chopped

Skin and deseed the tomatoes. You could use tinned tomatoes rather than fresh ones, although these may contain sugar. Put them in a saucepan. Finely chop the remaining vegetables and add to the saucepan, together with the tomato purée and two thirds of the stock, plus the basil. Bring to the boil and cook gently for 20 minutes or until the vegetables completely break up. (If you included the carrot and celery, this process will take a little longer.) If the mixture is too liquid, boil hard to reduce it. If it needs more liquid, pour in the rest of the stock. You can get a very smooth sauce by liquidising it or pushing the contents of the saucepan through a sieve.

Since this is such a useful sauce you might want to make a larger quantity and freeze portions of it.

Spicy Sauce
4 spring onions
1-inch piece of fresh root ginger
1 red chilli
1 small (200-220g) can of chopped tomatoes in juice
salt and pepper

Chop the spring onions and cook gently in a pan with a tiny bit of olive oil. Peel the root ginger and grate into the pan. Deseed and chop the chilli and add to the pan, cooking and stirring gently for a few minutes while adding the tomatoes. Let the sauce simmer and thicken. Season to taste and liquidise.

FRUIT SAUCES

Fruit sauces or purées are terrific with meat and fish dishes. They have a fresh, intense flavour that you simply do not get with a cream sauce, and fruit brings out the flavour of pork, game, and fish better than anything else. They should not be sweet – it is the tartness contrasting with the richness of the meat or fish that gives such a good combination. A splash of wine in your sauce helps things along – as do the cooking juices, carefully drained of any fat.

Blackberry Sauce
1 small punnet of really ripe blackberries
1 small cup of orange juice or water

Cook the fruit gently in the liquid until the blackberries disintegrate. Taste to see if you need to add a touch of sugar. (If the blackberries are really ripe, they will probably be sweet enough, particularly if you are using orange juice.) Liquidise, and rub through a sieve if you want to get rid of the pips.

This sauce is smashing with grilled duck breast but why not try it with pork or chicken?

Lemon juice is a great cooking standby. With the addition of a few chopped herbs and garlic it is a quick and classic marinade for grilled fish or chicken. Many lemon sauces designed to be a major part of dishes rely on butter or cream for thickening. These blunt the wonderful sharp lemon flavour – although a million chefs would probably disagree.

Try this simple version instead.

Lemon Tarragon Sauce
2 lemons
4 spring onions
150ml/5fl oz stock
fresh tarragon, chopped
a pinch of caster sugar
salt and pepper
1 teaspoon cornflour or arrowroot

Remove the peel and pith from the lemons and put the sliced flesh in a pan. Finely chop the spring onions. Add to the pan with the stock, most of the tarragon, and the sugar, and cook gently, adding salt and pepper to taste. Mix the cornflour with a little cold water to make a paste and stir into the sauce until it thickens. Strain the sauce and serve warm, adding more fresh chopped tarragon.

Variations

You can adapt this sauce in numerous ways – using garlic instead of tarragon, or other herbs such as rosemary or chervil, or just sticking to the lemon alone.

Passion Fruit and Lime Sauce

3 passion fruit
half a lime
1 small mandarin orange
1 tablespoon caster sugar
2 tablespoons water
½ teaspoon arrowroot

Cut the passion fruit in half and scrape the flesh into a pan. Peel and remove the pith from the other fruit and add the chopped flesh to the passion fruit, along with the sugar and the water, and cook gently for a few minutes. Mix the arrowroot with a little cold water to make a paste and stir into the sauce until thickened. If it is too liquid, boil hard to reduce; if too thick, add a little more water.

This is a nice fruity sauce to serve with pheasant or duck.

Gooseberries are one of the few fruits that you cannot get all the year round, which is sad considering that they grow in the UK and pop up in so many quintessentially British dishes. However, when you do find gooseberries in stock, grab them. They freeze well and make a lovely sauce to go with oily fish such as mackerel, herrings, and sardines. Try the sauce with salmon and trout, too.

Gooseberry Sauce

125g/4oz gooseberries
1 tablespoon caster sugar
a little water (or stock)

Wash the gooseberries and remove the stalk and the tufty brown bits at the base. Put in a saucepan, adding the sugar and water. Cook them gently until they lose their shape. Liquidise in a food processor and serve warm with the fish.

Apple sauce is a classic accompaniment to pork and can be easily made by cooking cored, peeled, chopped-up apples (cooking or eating) with a tablespoonful or two of water and then liquidising. As we have seen, you can find suitably lean cuts of pork – loin, trimmed chops, or fillet, for instance; the latter looks particularly good sliced like medallions on a plate in a pool of interesting sauce.

Why not try this more sophisticated version which really takes no more time to put together and which incorporates mustard – another flavour that goes so well with pork dishes.

Apple and Mustard Sauce
1 small onion
1 generous tablespoon wholegrain mustard
150ml/5fl oz unsweetened apple juice
1 eating apple

Finely chop the onion and cook gently in a saucepan with a light spray of oil until it just begins to brown. Add the mustard, then the apple juice, and boil until the ingredients reduce to a denser, more syrupy consistency. Peel, core and finely chop the apple. Add to the pan, letting it cook gently in the sauce for 2–3 minutes, before serving.

Ginger probably does not count as a fruit but it pops up time and time again in sauces, often combined with lemon or limes. It is wonderfully versatile – as good with salmon as with chicken or game – and here it combines well with soy sauce and honey to make a simple aromatic sauce.

Honey and Ginger Sauce

2 tablespoons cider vinegar
1 tablespoon light soy sauce
1 tablespoon honey
25g/1oz fresh root ginger, peeled and grated
zest and juice of half a lime
150ml/5fl oz water
2 teaspoons arrowroot

Put all the ingredients except the arrowroot in a pan and boil for 2–3 minutes. Drain, then return to the pan. Mix the arrowroot with a little cold water to make a paste and add it to the sauce, stirring as it comes to the boil and thickens.

VEGETABLE PURÉES

These are tasty and useful. They can be used as dips for raw vegetables, or thinned down with water and used as sauces.

Green Bean Purée (serves 4)

225g/8oz green beans (French or dwarf)
2 cloves of garlic
salt and pepper
squeeze of lemon juice
1/2 teaspoonful fresh savory or lemon thyme, chopped
2 tablespoonfuls low-fat fromage frais

Cook the beans until tender (either boil or steam). Then put them in a food processor with all the other ingredients and liquidise. This makes a particularly attractive sauce for pasta.

Watercress Sauce (serves 4)

1 bunch of watercress
juice of half an orange
1/2 teaspoonful finely chopped fresh green chilli

4 tablespoonfuls fromage frais
salt and pepper

Remove the tougher stalks from the watercress. Put all the ingredients in a food processor and liquidise. This sauce is delicious with fish or vegetables.

SALAD DRESSINGS

Salad dressings are a problem for slimmers. Inevitably you will want to eat more salads – and you should – but it may be hard to enjoy them without a decent dressing. Unfortunately *all* oils are very high in fat and calories – just because an olive oil comes from some amazing estate that everyone raves about doesn't mean it won't have exactly the same impact on your calorie intake as the equivalent amount of cheap old super-market vegetable cooking oil. It will.

There are low-calorie, low-fat, and fat-free dressings widely available in the supermarkets. The problem is that many of them have a nasty synthetic aftertaste – probably because they are, mostly, concocted out of nasty synthetics. If you find one you like – wonderful. If not, try to find your own instant substitute.

Lemon juice can be squeezed over salads (and meat and fish) to perk them up. So can **balsamic vinegars** – and the numerous other vinegars now appearing in the shops in great variety.

You can make your own **flavoured vinegars**, too, using wine vinegar.

- For **tarragon vinegar**, infuse the vinegar with the leaves for several weeks. Then strain off into a bottle. (There are no rules for the amounts to use in these vinegars – it all depends on how strong you want the flavour to be.)

- For **garlic vinegar**, put peeled and semi-crushed garlic cloves into the vinegar for a couple of weeks, then strain off.

Low-fat alternatives

Once you have lost the weight you want, you can experiment with some low-fat alternatives using low-fat yoghurt or fromage frais. The former tends to be runnier and more acidic than low-fat fromage frais, which has a creamier consistency and a milder flavour.

- If you want a creamier dressing for salads or vegetables, mix two tablespoonfuls (roughly 50g/2oz) of low-fat fromage frais with one teaspoonful of balsamic vinegar, some crushed garlic, and chopped herbs. This is particularly good with cooked vegetables or a potato salad.
- If you want a succulent sauce for chicken, mix one teaspoonful of mustard into two tablespoonfuls of fromage frais. For a spicier flavour, add a teaspoonful of curry paste or harissa (a hot paste widely used in Middle Eastern cooking and sold in the UK) to the fromage frais.

CHAPTER NINE

Exercise

GET TO GRIPS WITH EXERCISE

You can lose weight without taking any exercise. Any fool can starve themselves thin. But you will not be able to keep the weight off and eat normally at the same time if your lifestyle is sedentary. On the other hand, exercise alone will not produce the results you want if you carry on eating too much of the wrong kind of food.

In theory, exercise does speed up the process of weight loss because when you are more energetic you use up more calories. In practice it is quite disheartening to see how many miles you have to walk or run to work off the calories contained in a slice of cake or a Mars Bar. It's better not to contemplate the kind of list that shows you how many calories you use up in certain activities. Concentrate instead on the real reasons why getting to grips with exercise is a good idea.

WHY EXERCISE?

Almost all medical and scientific opinion holds that exercise improves health and the chance of a long life, but frankly, just being told this is not sufficient incentive for most of us to get out of our armchairs. There are some much better reasons why exercise is a good idea.

EXERCISE TONES THE BODY

Whatever your size, shape, or age, you are going to look much better if you are fit. A fit body is an attractive body. People who exercise as part of a weight loss plan will find that they can go down a dress size or two with the loss of only a few pounds. The reason for this is that muscle weighs more than fat and exercise builds more muscle as opposed to fat. The strengthened 'muscle corset' of your body, as it were, gives you a better outline.

> *People who exercise as part of a weight loss plan will find that they can go down a dress size or two with the loss of only a few pounds*

You can, of course, lose weight and go down a few dress sizes without exercising but you may, and probably will, still look flabby when you take your clothes off, no matter how much weight you lose. If you don't exercise a little as well as diet, you may not achieve the look you want.

Not even expensive plastic surgery can give you the look that you can get from just a little regular exercise. You can 'lipo-suck' pockets of fat away but you cannot buy the kind of muscle tone that comes from regular but modest amounts of exercise. The best things in life *are* free, but they take time and a bit of effort.

EXERCISE KEEPS YOU FLEXIBLE

As we get older, most of us become less active, although it sometimes feels as if we do so much more. Work – even just the business of getting to the office each morning – may be exhausting but as the years roll on and responsibilities increase, the opportunities to take exercise in our daily lives can be more difficult to find. Compared with our younger selves we may use up far fewer calories – just watch clips of clubbing teenagers dancing around and you will see why.

It is a fact that modern life requires us to be much less phys-ically active than our great-grandparents, who did not rely on cars to get them about or labour-saving devices in the home.

That is one of the reasons why so many of us are now over-weight in comparison with previous generations.

The way we live

It is not just that contemporary life reduces the amount of physical effort we expend in our daily lives. The way we live causes us actual damage because it encourages the body to position itself, and move, in totally unnatural ways. Hence the slumped shoulders and chin-first duck walks that you see everywhere, both of which are calculated to ruin the appearance of the slimmest person. Bad posture has a real impact on your figure – a prominent, distended-looking stomach, for instance, is often associated with certain kinds of back strain. Driving a car is one of the better-known recipes for back trouble. To that you can add sitting in an office, particularly if you are glued to a computer screen most of the day.

> Bad posture has a real impact on your figure

Not only are our lives physically restricted, shrunk almost, by the demands of daily life and work, but we may also be under a high degree of pressure and stress. This combination explains why so many of us suffer from problems such as backache and repetitive strain injury. Certain muscles are overworked, most are hardly used at all, and all the while the chemicals and hormones associated with stress whizz round our sedentary bodies. As a result just a seemingly slight or sudden movement of the arms or neck can spark off back trouble. The reason for this is that our range of physical movement has become restricted almost without our realising it. The idea of taking exercise, of course, becomes less and less attractive the more restricted our normal range of movement becomes.

We do need to exercise to offset these effects of twenty-first-century living. If we don't get enough exercise through our daily lives, we have to build it into our routines. Exercise ensures that you maintain a reasonable range and ease of movement all your life. It is also a good way of coping with stress. You will look and feel better as a result.

EXERCISE KEEPS YOU ENERGISED

OK, I hear you say that you are so busy that you have no time for exercise and in any case you are always too tired. One of the tricky things about contemporary life is that it wears you out, but uses up so few calories in doing so. The tiredness that you feel at the end of a day in the office is very different from the healthy exhaustion after a day spent digging the garden or in an energetic sport like sailing.

Physical exercise also seems to blunt the appetite, at least for a while. The irritations of the office have a quite different effect. You are more inclined to feel you want to eat something – to calm yourself down or perk yourself up. Part of this may be comfort eating – you treat yourself to something nice and tasty to boost your mood. If that something nice is a chocolate bar, it will probably give you a temporary lift, but that is all it will be – temporary.

> *Exercise actually gives you energy as well as using up calories*

Exercise, however, might be the best pick-me-up of all after or during a stressful day. At its most basic, exercise gets plenty of oxygen circulating round the whole system, which energises it. Exercise actually *gives* you energy as well as using up calories. If you exercise regularly you will find you can do so much more. Indeed, once you get used to exercising you will find that you start feeling fed up if you have to miss out on it for any length of time. This is because the process of exercising is believed to release certain hormones in the body that make you feel good – they can give you an exercise high.

Exercise and constipation

Exercise doesn't just work the muscles of your body, it helps all the vital internal functions as well. Exercise is particularly recommended if you suffer from constipation. Many overweight people do, and usually it is a sign that they are eating the wrong food and not taking enough exercise. They often find that if they change their diet and take up exercise their problem disappears along with the surplus fat.

EXERCISE HELPS YOUR METABOLISM

Exercise becomes very important when you are on a diet. One physical result of eating fewer calories is that the body should start using its fat stores – which is what we want. That process is speeded up by exercise. Another result of dieting is that the body may gradually get used to running on a smaller number of calories. So, even as you eat less and less, the rate of weight loss flattens out and may even stop. This is why starvation diets don't work and why people often find that they put on weight very fast once they return to 'normal' eating. The body compensates for its state of near-starvation and the metabolic rate – the rate at which you burn energy and calories – falls as the body adapts to surviving on less. The results can be very depressing for people caught up in this kind of yo-yo dieting.

One way to ensure that you do not fall victim to this problem is to make sure that your metabolic rate is raised by regular exercise while you are on a diet. If you are a hardened starvation dieter of many years' standing, you will find that concentrating on exercise, as well as eating properly, is going to be the only long-term solution to the damage you have inflicted on your system. The good news is that you can get it all back into balance.

The long-term impact

Some experts believe that the impact of exercise on your rate of energy use is not just a matter of using up more calories as you walk or jog around the place. They think that the effects are more permanent – that someone who takes regular exercise maintains this higher metabolic rate even after they have stopped exercising. Whatever, regular exercise helps to keep your metabolic rate normal when you go on a diet. The result will be that you don't fall into the dieter's trap.

GETTING STARTED

How you approach the problem of taking more exercise depends a great deal on your age and current level of fitness. What you are looking for is a real increase in activity that will ginger up your metabolism and hence your weight loss programme. Just as the body can adapt to different amounts of food, so it can get used to different levels of exercise. Bear this in mind when you hear conflicting advice about the value of different kinds of exercise.

There is no one way of approaching it. You must take an honest audit of your activity levels – and then build more of the right kind of exercise into your life. If, for instance, you dash around a great deal and feel stressed a lot

> *A good, long walk every day will get you fitter and help you lose weight*

of the time, you might find that a sociable sport (perhaps tennis, or a dance exercise class) will provide a good, fun balance. The right exercise is the form of exercise that you will be able to do on a regular basis with enthusiasm.

AN ACTIVITY DIARY

You have already done a food diary. Now do an activity diary marking the number of minutes you spend doing a physical activity each day. If you live a very sedentary life you can achieve a real difference quickly and easily. If you think you rely too much on your car, take any opportunity to leave it in the garage and walk instead. Little things like walking up the stairs to the office instead of taking the lift will be a big improvement, too.

If you have really not taken any formal exercise for a long time you are not likely to want to race into the nearest gym – and neither should you. Try taking good long walks instead (between two and five miles). Don't, however, believe the rubbish you see published claiming that a stroll along a country lane is as good as an energetic jog or a session in the gym. Lots of allegedly scientific reports claim to show this and the way that these reports are presented can be very misleading.

The truth is that if you haven't taken exercise for years a good, long walk every day will get you fitter and help you lose weight. It is easy, cheap, and you don't have to dress up for it. If you are used to being very inactive this can give you an instant improvement. However, if you are reasonably active in your daily life – for example, you have to run for the bus from time to time or you work in the garden at weekends – a nice country walk, while thoroughly worthy and enjoyable, is not really going to give your body the stimulus it needs to shed pounds. In order to help yourself lose weight, you need to upgrade your activity levels to something more energetic. This is the point at which those who are not inactive, but have done no formal or regular exercise, should start to think about what they can and should do to take more exercise.

WHICH EXERCISE?

In exercise, fashions change as they do in everything else. Not so many years ago, the health and fitness columnists were telling us to 'go for the burn' with Jane Fonda-style aerobic exercises. As a result there were many warnings about the effect on the joints of jumping-up-and-down exercise regimes, and low-impact aerobics such as mini-trampolining (or rebounding) became popular. Open the top fashion and beauty magazines now and you will find lots of journalists taking it easy on health farms, having a little detox session (fasting for a few days) in between trying a gentle introduction to yoga or some new Eastern adaptation of a martial art.

The first thing you should do is disregard anything like this you may have read. Most of it is written by people who couldn't run a mile even if their life depended on it and who count having an aromatherapy massage as a form of serious exercise. All kinds of exercise and therapy have their benefits, but not all of them will help you lose weight.

What to look for

Crudely, the test of any exercise is this:

- Does it make you feel as if you are getting out of breath? If so, it is having the desirable impact on your heart and lungs.
- Does it make you sweat? Great. This means that what you are doing is making your body and your system work harder, faster, and longer than it is used to. It is that effort, that stress on the body, that will help you to get fitter and lose weight.

But you must definitely *not* 'go for the burn' seventies-style or push yourself too hard too soon. If you have not exercised for a long time, you might feel you want a medical examination before you embark on an exercise programme. Start with a modest target and build up gradually. Once you start exercising regularly, you will know if you are doing too much or too little. There is no set target to aim for.

Now, an athlete would be operating positively below par if he or she ran just a mile a day. But for most of us running one mile would give our bodies a real wake-up call. The value of exercise can be relative, which is why it is nonsense to talk about the 'best' kind of exercise. The right exercise is the one your body needs to compensate for your lifestyle, or to balance your other activities. A competitive sportsperson will be superfit and have good technique but might well benefit from taking up a meditative stretching therapy such as yoga. The first need for someone who is sedentary, on the other hand, is to work up a sweat now and again. Leave the contemplative stuff until you can face up to looking at your navel!

> *The right exercise is the one your body needs to compensate for your lifestyle*

Sport

If there was an energetic sport that you enjoyed when younger – tennis, for instance – try to take it up again. The best kind of exercise is the exercise that you enjoy, and most sports are social events as well as competitive. It really is a matter of doing something you like – enjoying it ensures that you actually will do it and keep doing it.

Fast walking

Fast walking or power walking is very popular. Basically, this is rhythmic, purposeful striding and it can be very effective provided you don't mind looking a little ridiculous. You must make sure you wear the right shoes for fast walking or jogging to minimise the impact on your joints. You should wear trainers with well-cushioned soles rather than plimsolls.

Jogging

If you can't bear looking like one of those American women who stride along the beach wearing lipstick at eight in the morning, why not go the whole hog and try jogging? Slow jogging or fast walking – there is not much difference between them, really.

The right footwear is crucial. It helps if you can jog on a softer surface than a metalled road. You should not jog too far – ever. You should also do some basic leg stretch exercises to warm up your muscles before you start and when you have finished.

One of the results of the jogging craze was the increase in women running the marathon. Don't even think about it. The levels of training required are such that some women (and men) sustain an injury long before the starting pistol is fired. The hard athletic training required for a marathon can make you feel quite ill because it can have a damaging impact on your immune system. This amount of running can put a lot of pressure on your joints, and cause damage to the bones and muscles in the feet, legs, and groin as well, none of which is helpful to your activity levels in the long term. Injury may make it hard for you to exercise in the future which would be a great pity because jogging is one of the simplest and most accessible ways of helping weight loss and keeping fit.

You choose your own pace. You decide how far you want to go. It is simple and effective. It doesn't cost you anything once you have the correct footwear. One reason why jogging has had such a rotten press is the pure and simple fact that, apart from the sale of the shoes, there is not a huge amount of business to be generated out of it. Skiing is far worse for the joints but you can hardly open a weekend newspaper without seeing a favourable article or six about skiing, can you? But then, someone has holidays to sell you.

Cycling

Cycling is becoming very popular again, and rightly so. You must be careful about not putting too much pressure on your knees, and you should always wear a helmet. Cycling is, for many, more enjoyable than jogging but still achieves the object of getting you to take real exercise that gets you puffed out. And it can be quite a social activity, with weekend bicycling clubs active all over the country, which always helps the enjoyment and the motivation.

Rebounding

Rebounding, or mini-trampolining, has its fans. Basically, you jump up and down and do hops, skips, and jumps on a small, round trampoline about a foot off the ground. It is surprisingly good exercise – a form of jogging on the spot. Rebounders are now found in most sports shops. You can reduce the boredom factor by doing it to music. And it is nice and more effective to be able to exercise in the warm rather than have to turn out on nasty, rainy, or cold winter days. Lots of joggers use it as an alternative in very cold weather because freezing tempera- tures make the muscles more susceptible to injury.

Rebounding is particularly good because it shields the joints from hard impact but the physical effect is similar to jogging. The disadvantage is that you don't have a 'circuit' to get round. But if you are sufficiently motivated, sort out the old Abba CDs, get the kids out of the house, and off you go.

Swimming

Swimming is very good exercise provided you have the disci- pline to really thrash up and down hard and long enough. There is no stress on the joints. If you have a pool near where you work, a swim before or after work or at lunchtime a couple of days a week would be excellent. But if there are too many people in the pool bumping into you, it can be impossible to get a really good swim without interruption. Find out if there are any times when part or all of the pool is reserved for lane swimming.

Exercise classes

Dancercise, jazz dancing, step, and good old-fashioned aero- bics – there are plenty of exercise classes worth doing if you want to lose weight. It's important to check on who is giving them and what qualifications they have. There are a confusing number of different professional associations – some insist on actual qualifications and experience but some may just regis- ter anyone for a fee. As well as their experience you want to know details of the teacher's professional training. Whether it is in dance, gym, or aerobics, he or she should be able to produce evidence of training. The most basic recognised public qualification for fitness instructors and personal trainers is the NVQ Level 2. One option is to check the credentials of the teacher on the Register of Trainers and Teachers compiled by Exercise England (address: Solecast House, 13–27 Brunswick Place, London N1 6DX), which checks their credentials before putting them on the list.

Also, find out if the instructor covers the kinds of things that you want. In the first instance look for something with plenty of movement, like a dance class.

The kind of exercise class you choose may depend on what else you do. If you jog or play a sport such as tennis, a stretch class would be a better complement than something that just provided more aerobic training.

Gyms

Gyms are very good places for getting into shape, but they are expensive and the popular ones can often be crowded. You must make sure that you know what you are doing – all decent gyms have a mandatory induction course. You will feel more confident going to the gym if you have done a little regular exercise – jogging or rebounding perhaps – before you start.

HOW MUCH EXERCISE?

Any exercise is better than none, but you should aim to build up to around thirty minutes of high-energy activity three times a week. It needn't be the same kind of exercise. In fact, it is a good idea to vary your exercise since different activities exercise different muscle groups. Don't fall into the trap of becoming over-enthusiastic and taking *too much* exercise all at once. That is bad for your joints, and if you become overtired, you will just feel ill, not healthy. You will also risk injury.

CHAPTER TEN

Getting it off –
Keeping it off

BEING REALISTIC

In the first few weeks of your *No Fuss* diet and exercise regime you could lose anything between two and five pounds a week. It is important to remember that the most dramatic weight loss will be at the beginning. This is always encouraging, but don't run away with the idea that you can relax and ease up on the programme you have worked out for yourself. Weight loss will only continue if you keep a very sharp eye on what, and how much, you eat. And however disciplined you are, you must remember that once you are over the initial thrill of seeing quite a few pounds drop off, progress *will* slow down. If you manage to lose two to four pounds a month after the first few weeks, you are doing very well indeed.

The important thing is to persevere with your eating and exercise plans so that you lose all the weight you want – and keep it off. Here are some final tips that will help you develop, and stick to, sensible eating habits.

- **Don't** give up your diet just because you have had a bad day, eating all kinds of junk that you were never going to look at again. Just put it behind you and carry on.
- **Do** try to work out why you feel the need to suddenly break your diet, or binge. Some people react to emotional pressures by losing control of their eating; others overeat

through boredom. Find the cause and the next time the urge strikes, just go through the situation rationally. Breaking your diet is not going to solve the other problems that are the trigger for a bout of bad eating.

- **Don't** weigh yourself constantly. Our weight fluctuates quite a bit – we can be heavier at night than first thing in the morning, for instance. Weigh yourself once a week, at the same time of day. That's quite enough. The scales are just there as a reassurance. If you exercise regularly, you will see and feel a much greater difference than is likely to be measured on any scales.
- **Don't** skip meals. That is a sure-fire way to lose control over your diet.
- **Don't** go shopping when you are hungry. It is just too tempting.
- **Do** enjoy your food. Food is not the enemy. Take time to try something new that you think you will enjoy.

- **Don't** count calories. The whole point of the *No Fuss* approach is that you do not have to minutely examine everything you think of eating. Counting calories is miserable for you and everyone else, and it does not encourage you to adjust the balance of your diet in a way that will help you keep the pounds off, for ever.

- **Do** stick to the simple, general food formula – one meal fruit-based, one meal protein-based, one meal carbohydrate-based – on a day-by-day basis. Don't go on a fruit-only diet one day so that you can have two or three protein meals the next. You are just kidding yourself and your body will probably object.

- **Don't** talk about dieting. You will bore yourself and everyone else, and you will just start to feel deprived. The truth is that you are not deprived; you are actually trying to eat a truly balanced diet, and to balance your energy input and output.

- **Do** eat more slowly. Chew everything well. If you eat too fast, you will eat too much because it takes a bit of time for the brain to register that your stomach is full.

- **Don't** drink too much alcohol while you are trying to lose weight. It is very calorific and it's best if you can give it up altogether for a while. If you can't, stick to one glass of wine or the equivalent each day. Alcohol stimulates the appetite, so drink it with or after a meal, not before.

- **Don't** feel you have to rush out and buy lots of extra vitamins and supplements just because you are eating less food. The balanced diet suggested here should provide you with all the nutrients you need. If you were already taking supplements, just carry on with your usual intake.

- **Don't** scour the supermarket shelves for low-fat, no-fat, or low-calorie versions of high-calorie food. Much of what is sold as low-calorie is actually still highly calorific (the original version is worse, of course) and many low-fat dishes are loaded with sugar.

> **When you've found the eating pattern that suits your appetite and way of life, you will not feel that you are on a conventional diet at all**

A DIET FOR LIFE

Most of this book concerns itself with food – what to eat and what not to eat – but hopefully you will appreciate the huge benefits of exercise as well. It helps you to look and feel better in the most relaxed and healthy way possible.

Losing weight isn't easy. But once you have lost an initial few pounds and settled into your new routine of eating, you will find that it becomes a habit and you will feel less and less tempted to lurch back into the old undisciplined ways. When you've found the eating pattern that suits your appetite and way of life, you will not feel that you are on a conventional diet at all. You will feel less and less vulnerable to those feelings of deprivation and guilt that destroy so many attempts to lose weight. Instead, you'll have succeeded in moderating the way you eat – on a permanent basis.

All Orion/Phoenix/Indigo titles are available at your local bookshop or from the following address:

> Mail Order Department
> Littlehampton Book Services
> FREEPOST BR535
> Worthing, West Sussex, BN13 3BR
> *telephone* 01903 828503, *facsimile* 01903 828802
> *e-mail* MailOrders@lbsltd.co.uk
> (Please ensure that you include full postal address details)

Payment can be made either by credit/debit card (Visa, Mastercard, Access and Switch accepted) or by sending a £ Sterling cheque or postal order made payable to *Littlehampton Book Services*.
DO NOT SEND CASH OR CURRENCY.

Please add the following to cover postage and packing

UK and BFPO:
£1.50 for the first book, and 50p for each additional book to a maximum of £3.50

Overseas and Eire:
£2.50 for the first book plus £1.00 for the second book and 50p for each additional book ordered

----

BLOCK CAPITALS PLEASE

name of cardholder ....

delivery address
(if different from cardholder)

address of cardholder ....

....

....

....

postcode ....   *postcode* ....

☐ I enclose my remittance for £ ....

☐ please debit my Mastercard/Visa/Access/Switch (delete as appropriate)

card number ☐☐☐☐☐☐☐☐☐☐☐☐☐☐☐☐☐

expiry date ☐☐☐☐   Switch issue no. ☐☐

signature ....

prices and availability are subject to change without notice